KNIT AND NIBBLE

knitnibble.com

Cover images, plus images on pages 1, 16-17, 29, 82-83, 122-123 and 163 are credited to Anders Beier Photography. Image shoot location: the stunning Peckham Levels in London peckhamlevels.org @aoarchitecture

McINTOSH
PUBLISHING

Knit and Nibble™

First Edition

Author

James McIntosh MA

Photography and Images

© Anders Beier Photography 2018

andersbeier.com

Editor

Michelle Brachet MA

michellebrachet.co.uk

Food stylist

Sune Rasborg

sunerasborg.com

Published by

McIntosh Publishing 42 Denman Road, London, UK

mcintoshpublishing.com

ISBN 978-0-9934196-2-1

Printed by W&G Baird, Northern Ireland on FSC® paper. Supporting UK business and environmental awareness is important to us.

FSC
www.fsc.org
MIX
From responsible
sources
FSC® C016201

Watches by Charles BowTie

charles-bowtie.com

KNIT AND NIBBLE

James McIntosh

Edited by Michelle Brachet
Photography by Anders Beier
Food Styling by Sune Rasborg

To those who want to
enjoy a life in colour

The title of this book should be Happy, Knit and Nibble. It brought happiness back to its author, and it will give you weeks or even months of happiness. How many books can do that?

Edouard Cointreau
President
Gourmand World Cookbook Awards

knitnibble.com
#knitandnibble

KnitNibble

knitandnibble   @knitnibble

GET YOUR KNIT ON

Got to keep up: social media, styles, trends, exercise = pressure, pressure, pressure. And you can't find the correct emoji.

Hey, but you sleep when you're dead, right?

Ringing any bells? Well, these bells were ringing too loudly in my head. I had a busy job, lots of demands being self-employed: early mornings, late nights working, and too many international trips every few weeks.

And then, it's the weekend. Equally busy. A few years ago I was asked where the space was in my life. You know, that time when you can just switch off, watch the TV, have some '*me*' time. My life had become too busy. I was screaming inside, I was lost, I was struggling.

Then one day, at the age of 35, I could not get out of bed. I don't mean physically, I mean mentally. I had lost interest in everything I enjoyed and felt hopeless, sad, anxious, irritable. I had no motivation and zero energy. This was not me. I had always exuded a love for life, optimism and hope. Suddenly I felt helpless and scared, fear overcame me.

I'd heard about the positive benefits of Mindfulness, or to use its correct medical term Mindfulness Based Stress Reduction (MBSR). I was curious, and sceptical. How on earth could

spending time (that I didn't have) being '*mindful*' create more time in my day and less pressure on my life? But, I had nothing to lose; I gave it a go. Just a few minutes a day to start with, concentrating on my breathing and learning how to gently bring my mind to back to my breath when it wandered. It did not work. My brain was always busy, then I discovered that knitting and cooking could be practised in a mindful way.

I began to feel the benefits; a faint light began appearing at the end of that very dark tunnel I had been living in. Knitting removed my fear, gave me confidence and I learnt to **love myself**, **value Me** and make beautiful clothes for Me.

This quickly became my mindfulness; my therapy; my '*me*' time. And in time, hope and optimism started filtering back into my life.

My new life. Colourful again. That's my story.

And to you, a very warm welcome to a new life in happy, vibrant colour, in your clothes, food and most importantly in your mind.

James

Busy day?
Busy life?
Just busy, busy, busy?

The lure of the man cave:
- powerful
- seductive
- enticing
- inescapable

The only place where You can truly be You.

The grim realisation that reality is whispering in your ear.

Mind over matter, but you have to leave ... until next time.

The health and well-being benefits of Mindfulness practices are now increasingly recognised within published scientific literature. The main benefits quoted are:

- Stress and anxiety reduction
- Sleep improvement
- Prevention of relapse into depression
- Chronic pain reduction
- Better type 2 diabetes control
- Weight control
- Improvements in blood pressure

As well as other benefits relating to better personal relationships and work-life balance.

There have been randomised control trials and meta-analyses of these trials that now convincingly show these benefits are real. In addition, functional Magnetic Resonance Imaging (MRI) of the brain shows a marked increase of activity in parts of the brain - especially the frontal brain - where initiation and planning mainly occur. By increasing the activity, the ability to empathise, sharpen memory and improve attention, among other benefits, give an enhanced sense of self and return to a state of wellness. Hence, a link between the observed improvements and a likely mechanism through increased usage of the brain has been formally recognised. This scientific evidence has been a key trigger for the recent explosion in Western society of what is nearly an 8,000-year-old practice originating initially from yoga.

Traditional Mindfulness-based interventions, such as, Mindfulness meditation as used in Mindfulness Based Stress Reduction (MBSR), sometimes do not suit the busy modern Western (digital) resident. There is also a stigma of this being boring and old fashioned, unproductive or negatively spiritual. Hence in the West, alternative ways of

Knititation

Dr Thomas A. Ernst

Fellow of the Royal College of Physicians, London, UK

**Can't sleep?
Tired and run down?
Lacking energy?
Stressed at work?
Chronically ill?
Feeling anxious?
Or like me, in the past,
all of the above?**

creating benefits similar to meditation have been explored. One of them is the practice of knitting, or other crafts. The result: an increasing body of evidence with knitting mirroring in essence some of the above potential benefits of a mindful practise. Hence for those of us who cannot use the more stringently researched MBSR, knitting and other such crafts can be a fun and productive first step of a meditative creative process to explore the vast benefits of what MBSR has to offer. Couple this with a sense of 'self-love' when one's first knitted item is worn. I call this *Knititation*.

There are two key elements to MBSR:
1. To accept what happens in the present moment without judging, analysing or changing it.
2. To be aware when the mind wanders away from the present moment and gently directing it back to the present moment, over and over again.

During MBSR we generally use the breath as the present moment anchor. In Knititation this anchor is simply a new stitch, which is also in the present moment. The advantage of the practice of Knititation is that the speed can be chosen to suit the business of one's own mind, once the basis of the practice (craft) has been mastered. Just simply follow what James has written to masterfully acquire this art.

This book is laid out like the practice of Mindfulness: start with small items to learn the respective art, building up over time to complete significant achievements; e.g. less anxiety and a completed jumper. If you stopped trying to walk after your first fall you would still be crawling now. The old adage of falling off the horse, but getting back on is what is important. Hence, it is good and healthy to

choose an art that you can persist with despite initial setbacks. James's first jumper was not particularly en vogue, but it was a trophy that he will cherish for the rest of his life, even if it lives at the back of the wardrobe.

Knitting, possibly like the practice of MBSR, sparks the neurons and neurotransmitters and all of the other complex chemical and physiological items that make up our very multiplex and evolved brains. The practice of either to the brain is like turning on the lights of a Christmas tree.

So what is the outcome? I will let James speak for himself. Through Knititation he achieved:
- Better sleep
- Less smoking, with a clear view to giving up
- No more anxiety and gone are the winter blues
- Easier stress management
- Return of normal energy levels
- Creativity in abundance

But best of all, his life is colourful again.

The Sirdar Story

Mention the name **Sirdar** to a knitter and they instantly smile knowing the quality of the yarns and knitting patterns produced. Sirdar *is the* go-to brand worldwide for yarn. But there is more to Sirdar than this. An inspiration of colour and style, Sirdar keep up to date and set new trends in the global hand-knitting market.

With a history of nearly 180 years promoting the best of Great British craft, generation after generation have worn clothes knitted from Sirdar yarn and patterns. Most likely you have too - from a lovingly knit baby outfit in **Sirdar Snuggly** to a jumper from their vast collection of yarns.

Tom, Henry and Fred

A gentle stroll around Wakefield in West Yorkshire, England, shows the history of Sirdar. Street names honouring many of the company directors surround the huge yarns mill and design house that Sirdar has occupied since 1890. In fact, Wakefield has been notable for yarn since the Middle Ages, and this continues right up to today. In 1880, a generation into the Industrial Revolution, Tom and Henry Harrap started to sell yarn fibres before passing the company to Tom's son Fred.

Uniting the British Army to 007

Knowing he had a quality product, Fred adopted the name '*Sirdar*' as a sign of strength, which meant '*leader*' after the title given to Lord Kitchener as '*Sirdar of the Egyptian Army*'. Sirdar started to sell their yarns to independent retailers and by 1934 produced the first Sirdar knitting patterns.

Men, women, children and babies have since worn garments developed by Sirdar. During wartime, Sirdar produced patterns entitled '*More Comfort for the Forces*', encouraging help on the Home Front. Furthermore, arguably the most famous model for Sirdar was Sir Roger Moore, AKA 007.

A Family Affair

As the years rolled by, Sirdar grew from strength to strength and the company passed to Mrs Jean Tyrell, Tom Harrap's granddaughter.

Mrs Tyrell was a visionary. She introduced the quality products of Sirdar to the hand knitter by being the first hand-knitting company to editorially feature in fashion magazines. Pioneering the growth of Great British textiles, she was awarded an OBE (Order of the British Empire) for her lifetime's achievements.

Sirdar is currently a part of the **DMC, Sirdar, Wool and The Gang Group**. Global distribution and brand strength has never been stronger, yet the history and hallmarks of what make Sirdar so special to the knitter remain.

Design House: the Sirdar Knitting Room

Straddling design concepts as the decades passed, Sirdar has had its own in-house design department from 1934. An award-winning team of knitwear designers, currently led by Julie Langham, have produced thousands of knitting patterns over the years encompassing all fashion trends: from mohair and batwings in the 1980s to baggy jumpers of the 1990s and more fitted items for current clothing and homeware trends.

Sirdar is the only yarn provider in the UK with such a design department in-house. Everything is hand knitted, then checked at least three times. The commitment to the knitter is a top priority for Sirdar. All designs are both a pleasure to knit and stylish to wear.

Sirdar has a strong belief that knitting patterns should be easy to follow and correct; pattern writing being a slow and complex process. The design team work at all levels of the supply process, from choosing yarns for the current portfolio to creating designs and testing the patterns. A hive of colourful activity, Sirdar take great pride in their work.

The process being:

- Initial design samples and knitted swatches
- Pattern writing
- Maths checking
- Sample knit
- More maths
- Photography
- Pattern layout

Yarn Ranges

Sirdar has a long list of yarn ranges within their portfolio including yarns for babies, classic yarns and fashion yarns in a plethora of colours, thickness and types. Cottons, bamboo, rayons, acrylics and the truly gorgeous high-end Sublime range comprising of Extra Fine Merino wool, alpaca wool and baby cashmere. Designs across all brands include tweeds, striped yarns and cake yarns.

sirdar.co.uk
sublimeyarns.com

SIRDAR

Yarns by Sirdar

Five different ranges of yarn have been used in this book, giving a total of 106 yarn colours, allowing for nearly ¾ million colour choices of garments from my patterns.

To make natural yarn, the fibres need to be carded (a combing process that removes impurities like seeds and vegetable matter) before being spun, dyed and then wound into balls.

Sirdar Cotton DK

A sustainable and recyclable high quality Egyptian cotton.

Made from long cotton strands of high quality, Sirdar Cotton DK is strong, soft and resistant to stress. It is mercerised to create a subtle sheen, making an extremely high quality yarn. The colours in this range create gorgeous projects for garments to wear and items for the home that are resistant to pilling. The stitches show great definition when knit and it's machine washable up to 40°C too. Made of 100% cotton, with the correct care, it can last for many years.

SIRDAR

KNIT & CROCHET

COTTON DK

BEAUTIFUL COLOURS BY THE
SIRDAR DESIGN STUDIO

501 Mill White

500 Black

502 Vanilla

504 Light Taupe

509 Darling Bud

510 Galore Red

514 French Navy

515 Bluebird

516 Tranquil

519 Cool Aqua

520 Grey Dawn

527 Cool Blue

531 Citrus

533 Seashell

537 Parchment

540 Mediterranean Blue

526 Blossom

538 Breaking Waves

511 Hot Pink

530 Pomegranate

512 Black Violet

532 Lotus

539 Terracotta

Sirdar Harrap Tweed

A yarn of heritage - named after the Harrap brothers, founders of Sirdar.

A range of rich tweeds inspired by the landscape of Yorkshire, the home of Sirdar. Machine washable at 40°C and perfect for all sorts of knitted projects. Made from a blend of fibres: nylon, wool, acrylic and viscose, it's incredibly strong and has a soft feel. Available in both DK (Double Knitting) and Chunky weights; both products are the same, except the Chunky is nearly twice as thick.

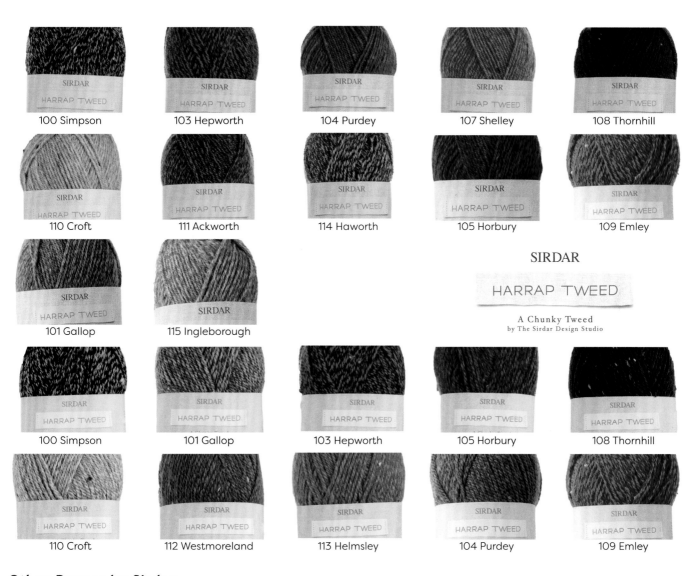

100 Simpson	103 Hepworth	104 Purdey	107 Shelley	108 Thornhill
110 Croft	111 Ackworth	114 Haworth	105 Horbury	109 Emley
101 Gallop	115 Ingleborough			

SIRDAR

HARRAP TWEED

A Chunky Tweed
by The Sirdar Design Studio

100 Simpson	101 Gallop	103 Hepworth	105 Horbury	108 Thornhill
110 Croft	112 Westmoreland	113 Helmsley	104 Purdey	109 Emley

Other Ranges by Sirdar

With a yarn type for every knitting and crochet project, Sirdar has it all: Snuggly baby yarns, self striping, alpaca, bamboo, silk, acrylic, rayon, cashmere, fashion, super chunky, supersoft, faux fur, chenille, mixed fibre, cake yarns and flecked yarns.

Other brands in the Sirdar portfolio as well as **Harrap Tweed** and **Sublime** are **Hayfield**, **Country Style** and **Snuggly**. Snuggly is the UK's favourite yarn brand for baby knits.

Sublime

An exquisite natural yarn collection in beautiful colours for great designs.

Sublime is Sirdar's luxury range and comes in many different yarn types. Sublime Extra Fine Merino DK and Worsted yarns are both made from pure extra fine Merino wool. DK or Double Knitting is a traditional UK weight and Worsted is a traditional USA weight (thicker than DK, but thinner than Aran). Merino is a special breed of sheep that grow fine wool. With Sublime, an extra fine fibre diameter of 18.6 microns is used, resulting in the softest yarn that is a pleasure to knit with. Machine washable at 30°C.

extra fine merino wool dk

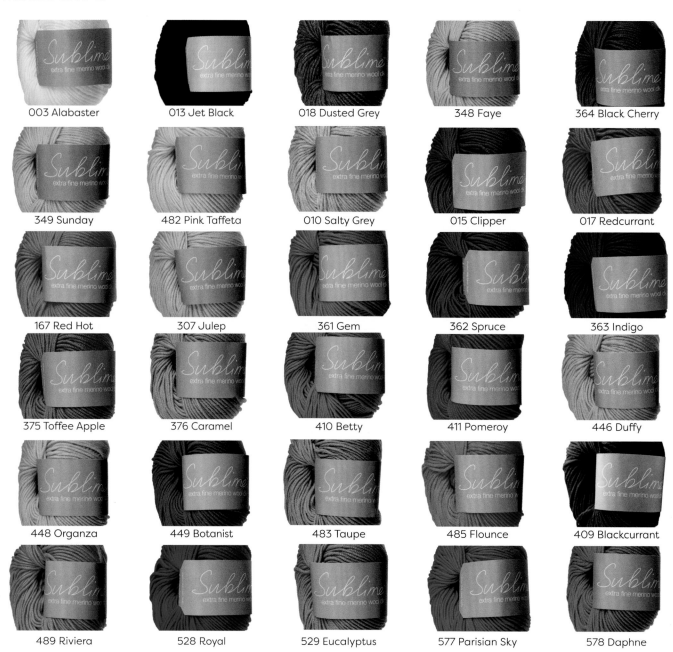

003 Alabaster	013 Jet Black	018 Dusted Grey	348 Faye	364 Black Cherry
349 Sunday	482 Pink Taffeta	010 Salty Grey	015 Clipper	017 Redcurrant
167 Red Hot	307 Julep	361 Gem	362 Spruce	363 Indigo
375 Toffee Apple	376 Caramel	410 Betty	411 Pomeroy	446 Duffy
448 Organza	449 Botanist	483 Taupe	485 Flounce	409 Blackcurrant
489 Riviera	528 Royal	529 Eucalyptus	577 Parisian Sky	578 Daphne

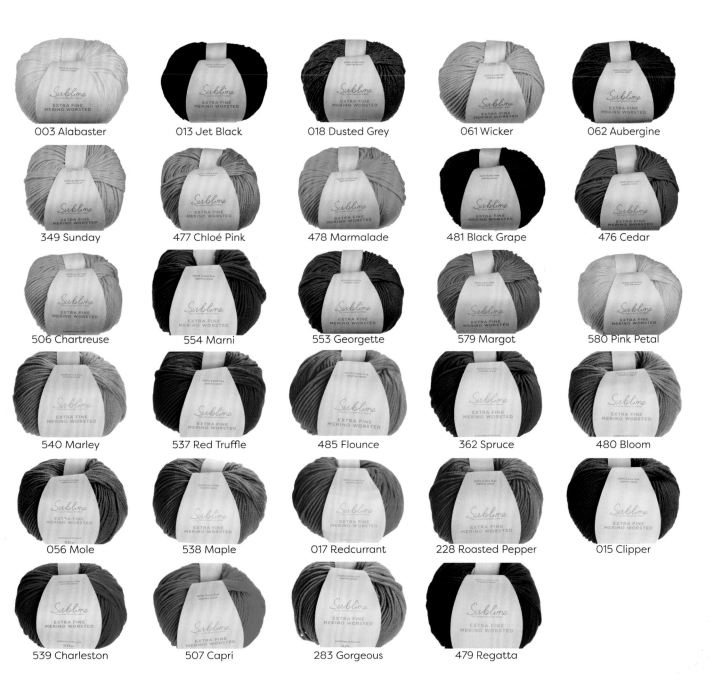

003 Alabaster	013 Jet Black	018 Dusted Grey	061 Wicker	062 Aubergine
349 Sunday	477 Chloé Pink	478 Marmalade	481 Black Grape	476 Cedar
506 Chartreuse	554 Marni	553 Georgette	579 Margot	580 Pink Petal
540 Marley	537 Red Truffle	485 Flounce	362 Spruce	480 Bloom
056 Mole	538 Maple	017 Redcurrant	228 Roasted Pepper	015 Clipper
539 Charleston	507 Capri	283 Gorgeous	479 Regatta	

KNITTING PhD
PROJECT
HALF DONE

Knit....

How to do it and what you need to create a bespoke you:

1. 2 x KnitPro needles
2. A ball of Sirdar yarn
3. Press the accelerator

Made to Measure

First find a tape measure ...

Not the one from a tool box that's made of metal - it won't bend round the body that well.

Find a non-metallic, preferably fibreglass one. Stand up straight, shoulders back, and with some help measure around your chest, across where one's nipples are would be best. Not too tight, enough for two fingers to ease between the tape and your body. Take a note of the size.

Work in either centimeters or inches, whichever you prefer; the patterns in this book are written for both. Best not to mix measuring units though, so stick with either centimetres or inches as you go. This corresponds to the table below for the **Fit Chest** measurement. The **Actual Size** is the size the finished item will actually be. The **Full Length** is the length from the cast-on edge to the top of the garment. **Sleeve Length** is the length of the sleeves, but this can be adjusted as stated in the knitting patterns if you have slightly longer or shorter arms.

It's a good idea to measure the length of the sleeve, just to ensure the body sizes stated above are correct for you. To do this, simply measure along the inside of the arm. This does not get complicated as one knits, the patterns will tell you where to increase or decrease if you want the sleeves a different length.

It's important to measure accurately, as the knitting patterns for the jumpers and tank tops in this book will turn out to these sizes if your tension square is correct. See page 49. If you find your size is between chest sizes, always round up to the bigger size.

Next, decide what colour gingerbread person you are from the diagrams below.

All of the jumpers in this book will follow the same gingerbread colour coding.

Sizes

To Fit Chest	cm	**97**	102	107	**112**	117	122
	in	**38**	40	42	**44**	46	48
Actual Size	cm	**97**	103	108	**112**	117	123
	in	**38**	40 ½	40 ½	**44**	46	48 ½
Full Length	cm	**68**	70	72	**73**	74	75
	in	**26 ¾**	27 ½	28 ¼	**28 ¾**	29 ¼	29 ½
Sleeve Length	cm	**47**	48	48	**49**	50	51
	in	**18 ½**	19	19	**19 ¼**	19 ¾	20

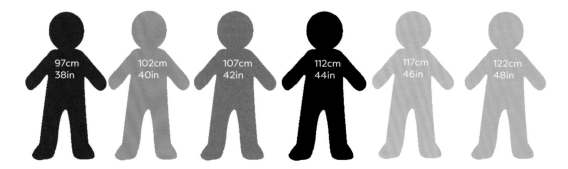

97cm 38in · 102cm 40in · 107cm 42in · 112cm 44in · 117cm 46in · 122cm 48in

Equipment...

They say a bad workman blames his tools

Here's how to find the best tools for knitting

That way, you will be a great workman, and one who can knit too

Choosing Yarn

Choosing yarn can be a very pleasurable experience. From giving a ball a gentle squeeze to privately savouring the softness, as well as having an electrifying inspiration for a particular colour combination.

Keen knitters have what they call their 'stash': an over abundance of yarn, hidden in cupboards, under the bed and even at the bottom of laundry baskets. Instagram is full of intelligent places to store one's stash.

#showusyourstash

Dye Lot

When fibres are dyed, different weights of yarn are dyed depending on the yarn brand's order. Some colours of yarn will sell better than others, however, as fashions change and more yarn is ordered, new lots of yarn need to be produced. For natural fibres like cotton and wool (including Merino) the fibre is dyed and then spun into yarn; this gives an even colour. Rayon, acrylics, nylons and other man-made and synthetic fibres are dyed during the fibre production process. Each batch will be consistent in colour, however, different batches could have subtle differences. After all, it's a natural product and not a CMYK or Pantone absolute.

For this reason it's best to buy all of the yarn stated on a knitting pattern in one go, ensuring they all have the same dye lot. This can be easily checked by the 'lot' number printed next to the shade number on the ball band. With popular shades, it may be difficult to find a dye lot match later on: another reason to keep the ball band for reference.

Weights of Yarn

DK, Worsted, Chunky - what's the scoop?

Yarn comes in many thicknesses, known as weights (not mass) termed as 'ply'. In singular form, a ply is a single strand of yarn, so for example, 4 ply is traditionally made of 4 strands of fibre. Double Knitting or DK may be referred to as 8 ply at times. As yarn technology has developed, the thickness of a single ply is not always as obvious in terms of the weight (mass) of the ball, as some very thick yarns may have a lower mass than thinner yarns.

What is important is how the yarn knits: to that end, the tension square is very important. Many yarn manufacturers determine the weight of yarn by noting the tension square: 22 stitches by 28 rows knit on 4mm needles resulting in a 10cm (4in) square determines a Double Knitting or DK yarn. You may notice some DK yarns have a longer length of yarn in a ball than others. This all depends on the yarn fibre, spinning method etc., so a greater length of yarn per ball weight is not always better value.

Yarn weights have different names across the world, as a rough guide:

UK	USA	Australia
1 ply	Laceweight	2 ply
2 ply	Fingering / Superfine / Baby	3 ply
3 ply	Sock	3 ply
4 ply	Sport	5 ply
DK	DK / Light Worsted	8 ply
Aran	Worsted / Afgan	10 ply
Chunky	Bulky / Craft / Fishermmans	12 ply
Super Chunky	Super Bulky	14 ply

WARNING

THIS CAN BE ADDICTIVE

Types of Yarn

Yarn comes in all sorts of different variants, not only different weights, but also fibres. Each fibre has its positives and negatives: some natural, others man-made and some synthetic. Fibres can be mixed together, or blended to use the attributes of one fibre to complement another. For example, a wool and nylon mix gives strength to wool, yet allows the yarn to feel soft and warm. Yarn technology has come a long way over the years and items with an acrylic mix like Sirdar Harrap Tweed can be hard-wearing and soft too.

Natural Yarns

Sheep Wool

Soft, natural and strong.

The king of knitting yarn, this natural product is strong, durable, elastic and feels soft against the skin. Not only will wool hold dye well, it also holds its shape when knitted and sewn into a garment. Due to its natural purpose, wool also has great insulation properties and will keep you warm. It won't form little bobbles (called *pilling*) as readily as some synthetic fibres may.

Not all wool is the same - different breeds of sheep produce different types of wool. Lambswool is soft, Merino has long fibres that produce a luxurious sheen when knit, and Shetland wool is very strong and fine.

Wool that is machine washable or suitable for the tumble dryer has been treated to avoid shrinkage. Some people may find wool a little itchy and rough; this should settle with washing and wear.

As you knit through this book you will discover my love for Sirdar Sublime Extra Fine Merino wool - and hopefully agree with me - the soft bouncy yarn adds a certain little je ne sais quoi to knitting. Machine washable too. Trés magnifique.

Cotton

Crisp stitch definition holding rich colours.

A natural product resulting in a heavy yarn that can droop due to the weight. This can be fixed, however, as cotton is rather resilient and comes back into shape after washing. The absorbency of the cotton fibre allows for a rich, deep colour palette of dyes, resulting in stunning knitted projects.

Cashmere

Snug and lush.

A beautiful wool that is synonymous with luxury. Delicate to the touch with a gorgeous soft finish made by woven short fibres, which are not as itchy as wool, yet still provide warmth. Made from the fibres of the under layer of a goat's coat, supersoft varieties of cashmere come from goats high up in mountains like the Himalayas and Mongolia. A single goat may only produce 200g (about 4 balls) of cashmere per year, which is why it is so expensive.

Alpaca

Warm in bitter weather.

A luxurious hard-wearing yarn from the cutest animal on the farm. It has a silky feel that is more resilient than sheep wool, with amazing insulation properties.

Silk

A great investment for a classic garment.

Soft and lightweight that is, as per its name, silky against the skin and beautiful to knit. A garment knitted in silk yarn will be very sexy when worn. Hard-wearing, if tightly spun.

Mohair

Notable for its fluffy 'halo' effect.

This goat yarn has a unique frizzy appearance and is not the easiest to knit with. Looks great when making oversized jumpers; reminiscent of the *Brit Punk* era.

Bamboo

Silky vegetable matter.

Flexible fibres from within a bamboo cane; these grass fibres knit and wear like silk.

Angora

An ethical question.

Beautifully soft, however, the harvesting of this yarn poses strong ethical questions.

Synthetic Yarns

Hard-wearing for everyday garments.

Ideal for a *'jumper about the house'* as it can be washed by machine with little care required.

Some knitters, however, find this yarn too uncomfortable to wear. The stitches may also cling to the knitting needles and not slide easily. Finished garments may pill and if steam ironed may loose elasticity resulting in a badly shaped garment. They are, however, thoroughly hard-wearing.

Acrylic

Affordable and machine washable.

A synthetic fibre; a sort of plastic, but don't let that put you off. Firstly, these yarns are hypoallergenic and the colour palettes are stunning.

This low-maintenance fibre may not insulate the body as well as wool, but it's cheap, easy to knit with and great for beginners.

Blended Yarns

The best of both worlds.

Combining natural and synthetic, strength and texture marry to create some truly fabulous yarns. Cashmere socks may sound delightful, but they will lack the elasticity required to keep the socks pulled up and the durability for the friction they will have to endure. Blended yarns of wool, used for socks as a perfect example, bring the strengths of different yarns together.

Baby Yarns

Gentle and hard-wearing.

Specific yarns for babies (like the **Sirdar Snuggly** range) are blended to make soft yarns that don't irritate delicate baby skin as pure wool may.

Baby yarns are designed to be machine washed.

Textured Yarns

Great for making a statement.

Big and chunky, fine and embellished or a yarn of uneven thickness. Furry, shiny, and utterly outrageous yarns are covered in this category.

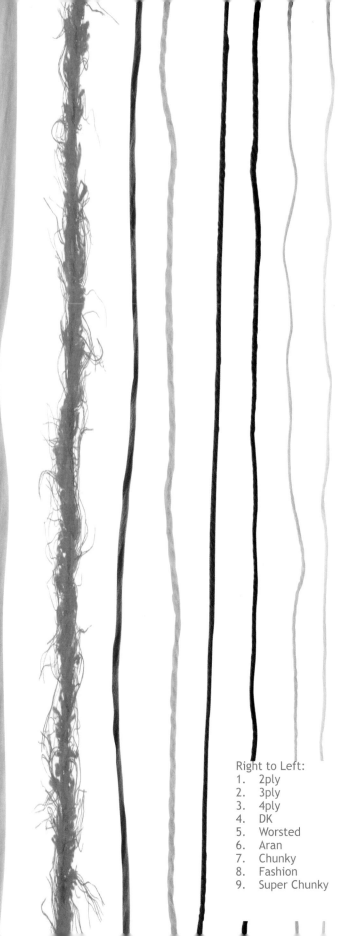

Right to Left:
1. 2ply
2. 3ply
3. 4ply
4. DK
5. Worsted
6. Aran
7. Chunky
8. Fashion
9. Super Chunky

Machine Washable.
Dry flat.
Reshape whilst wet.

10x10cm
28 rows 4x4in
22 sts

USA 6 UK 8
4mm
4mm
8 UK-F5 US

www.sublimeyarns.com

100% extra fine merino

Sublime

extra fine merino wool dk ™

50g*
116m / 127yds
approx

Lot 14061

Shade 0015

In accordance with
B.S. 984 50g nett at
standard condition.
Made in Italy.
Made for Sublime
under licence in Italy.

How to Read a Yarn Label

Labels on yarn tell you all about the product:
the size of the yarn; care and washing
instructions; what needles to use.

1. Laundry instructions

2. Yarn tension

3. Recommended needle size for the tension
   square that the knitting patterns for the
   yarn are designed for

4. Yarn fibre composition

5. Yarn name

6. Weight of ball

7. Length of yarn in ball

8. Dye lot

9. Shade number

Substituting Yarn

If you buy a yarn that is recommended in a
knitting pattern, the only thing you really need
to do is to choose the colour and check the
care and washing instructions. If, however,
you would like to use a different yarn, then
it's important to get the right yarn for the
intended project, i.e. replace DK with DK or
Chunky with Chunky. You have to knit with
what the pattern says. Don't forget to check
the tension. See page 49.

DON'T TANGLE MY BALLS

Colour

Emotions shine through in colour. It can be used and manifested to tell stories in many ways, to show mood, reality, braveness and abstracts in ways that words cannot. Professionally it's called art.

Colour has its own language, rather a set of sensibilities developed to allow colour to speak and colours to story tell. From neutral tones, to brighter spectrums, monochromes and splashes; colour is a journey, a train with no stations but curves in the railway line; an evocation of reality, joie de vivre, a caffeine or sedative, sobriety or twilight; a psychological visual pathway with its own aroma. Welcome to bespoke you.

Within this book you will find thousands of possible colour combinations from the Sirdar spectrum for all the knitting patterns. Using the tools below, design your own, knit, and post on Instagram.

#knitandnibble

Look Around

Inspire yourself. Do something you would not normally do. Find inspiration on the journey of striking something off your bucket list. A walk in the park, a sunset, the colour of an unwaxed Sicilian lemon, the inside of a pomegranate. Use all of your senses and translate these findings to yarn colours, ensuring you look at them in different light sources. Knit a swatch of colour and share it with friends. Comfortable colours originate from nature, statement colours are more digitally derived.

Colour Wheel

Artistic architectural movements breathe life into urban spaces to create a higher echelon of the living environment. The Bauhaus movement in Germany resulted in the production of a colour wheel: a statement of primary, secondary and tertiary colours in 12 segments and how they relate to each other in a circular interdependence.

Split into quarters the wheel has 3 primary colours: red, yellow and blue. Just like letters in the Latin alphabet, they exist alone and cannot be created. If mixed, secondary colours develop from this: red and yellow produce orange; blue and yellow make green; and red and blue create violet. Mix again, and other shades start to develop ad infinitum. Adding black and white now gives us a visual palette to work with.

Once the colour wheel is understood, the following ensures colours will work together:

- Opposites attract for 2 colour options giving dynamic colour energy.

- A colour chosen from each of the 3 points on an equilateral triangle go together.

- Analogous colours sit next to each other on the wheel. If one colour is chosen to be a base colour, any of the hues from the colour options next to it will complement rather harmoniously.

- Tetradic colours are 4 colours that work together in 2 complementary pairs giving rich colour combinations. Draw a rectangle within the colour wheel; the four colours are identified by each corner of the rectangle.

Warm and Cool Colours

Split the wheel in half and one side is expressed as warm colours, which include red, yellow, orange, brown. On the other side cool colours are green, blue and violet. The easiest way to remember the difference between warm and cold colours is to think of warm colours as a summers day and cold colours as an overcast day. A garment knit in warm colours will have a zing of life, whilst the same garment knit in cool colours will have a certain sobriety: active or receding moods respectively if you like.

Tones

Black and white used together can produce a certain energy to colour, block a segment or state an artistic direction. Used singly, black and white can transform a knitting pattern in colour to a safer 'classic' item of apparel. This shows just how style can be influenced by not only the shape of a garment, but also the colour and tone of it.

Adding white to a colour makes a tint; adding black produces a shade.

Confidence, Not Colour Theory

The use of colour in a scientific way, much has been written and debated on the subject. It's all subjective, of course, and if your choice is pleasant to you, then you will wear your knitted item with confidence. Surely confidence of the wearer is the true definition of style, rather than the spectral light wavelengths emitted.

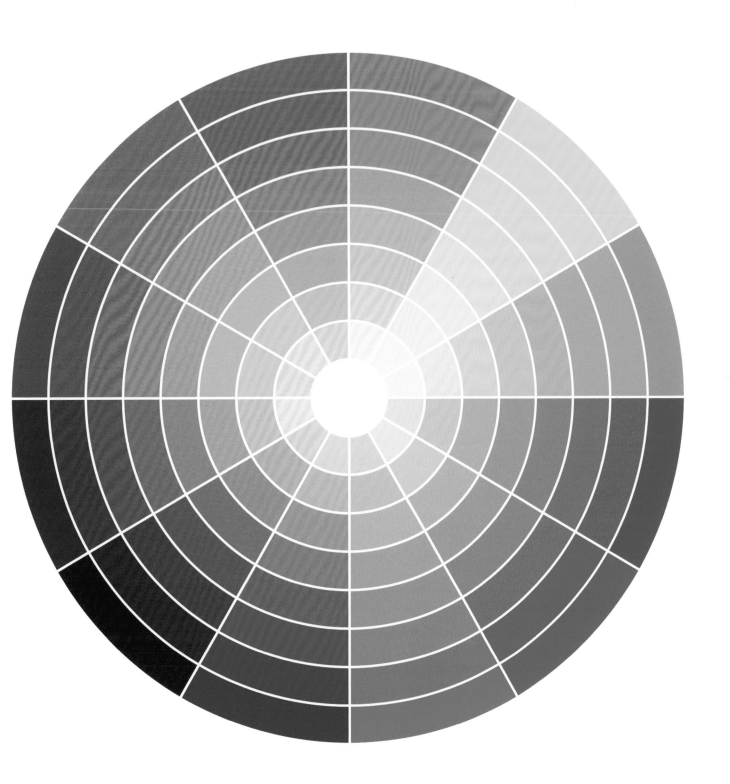

The Colour Wheel

Knitting Needles

And other bits and bobs you will need

Choosing Knitting Needles

Many different types of needles are available. Whether wood or plastic, single ended or double ended, choosing needles is all a matter of personal taste and what you find most comfortable.

Different lengths of needles are available. Some people like to knit on longer needles, others on shorter ones. Use whatever is right for you and the size of your knitting project. Do remember that all stitches should fit comfortably on your chosen needles; to avoid stitches falling off, the needle should not be too crammed with stitches.

Needle size in knitting patterns refers to the diameter of the needle, not the length of the needle and different countries have different measurement systems. In this book knitting needles are measured in millimetres (mm). Old Imperial British and American sizes can be converted for the sizes used in the patterns in this book from the following table. Needle sizes may vary slightly from manufacturer to manufacturer. Square needles are measured across the diagonal; round needles across the diameter.

Single Pointed Needles

As the name suggests, they have just one point for knitting with a stop at the other end. The needle size will usually be printed on either the stop or on the side of the needle. Single pointed needles are used for knitting flat objects. A row is knit from one needle to the other and then back again, usually from left to right.

Single pointed needles are the easiest needles to start knitting with. All patterns in this book use single pointed needles.

Double Pointed Needles (DPN's)

A needle with 2 pointed ends that can be used for either flat or circular knitting.

For circular knitting using a DPN: these needles come in sets of 4 or 5 and negate the need to turn your work at the end of knitting a row in order to start the next row.

The size of the needle is generally printed on the side. It may be easier to keep these needles together with an elastic band when storing. DPNs are great for making socks, sleeves and knitting a round neckband, or any other items where a seam is not appropriate.

First time using DPN's can feel a little fiddly, so it's always best to have a practise first.

Circular Needles

One long needle with 2 pointed ends joined with either a plastic or metal wire; they also come in different lengths.

Many knitters prefer these to single pointed needles because you can knit in the round as well as back and forth in straight lines. Many find these best for travelling, especially if knitting on a bus, train or plane (always check with the airline first) as one's elbows don't stick out so much as opposed to when using straight needles.

Interchangeable Circular Needles

A special type of circular needle with ends that can be removed to change the size of the needle end. They take up less space than a full set of needles. When buying, brands like KnitPro are highly regarded as they have worked hard to develop a seamless join between the needle and the wire. Some brands' needles can catch the stitches on the join between the needle and wire resulting in stitches not flowing as easily when knitting.

Millimeter	Old UK	USA
3	11	3
3.5	9	4
4	8	6
4.5	7	7
6.5	3	10 ½

Knitting Needle Material

Needles can be made from many items: wood, bamboo, ebony, plastic, aluminium, steel and other items too like carbon fibre. There is no best material; each needle material has different attributes. It's all about individual preference. 30cm needles are best for beginners.

The point of the end of the needle is worth considering; some are sharp and others are blunt. A blunt needle is harder to insert into thinner yarn, yet a sharper one can split stitches.

Wood and bamboo needles are great for beginners: they are less slippery than plastic and metal needles, meaning the stitches won't slip off the end so easily.

The only thing that really matters when choosing needles is what is good for you and easy to knit with. It's also always good to have a mix of needles of different sizes, lengths and materials in your collection. Technically speaking, ergonomics and torque are what matter when choosing needles:

- **Ergonomics**

  The design for efficiency and comfort when working stitches is different for everyone.

- **Torque**

  Being one of the strongest materials, metal needles can hold greater torque (force applied in an arc to cause rotation), which is perfect for supporting large, heavy projects like blankets and throws preventing bending or breaking. Knitting the neckband for a jumper can force pressures onto a bamboo needle and bend it. Stronger needles may be required to finish a project even though lighter weight ones were used during the main knitting.

Metal

Speed and Strength.

Stainless steel, aluminium, brass, powder coated, nickel plated and alloys of the aforementioned are all covered within this classification and all give the classic '*clicking of needles*' sound. And, ooh they are shiny!

Rigid and inflexible, some knitters find they may cause fatigue in the hands and wrist joints. The great positive with metal needles: they have less surface friction so stitches will slide easier along the needles; a slick runway for freshly knit stitches. Also, not all metal needles have cylindrical shafts. Who says you can't fit a square into a round hole? Powder coated and brass needles are the least slick of the metal needle fraternity; stainless steel sit somewhere in the middle; while nickel coated are the cool runnings bobsleigh of stitch fiddling. On that and a final note, some knitters find metal needles cold to the touch.

The KnitPro Story

Sadly, not everyone has the best opportunities in life and that's where KnitPro are brilliant; they help to knit equality into society. Based in India, KnitPro help women in all manner of ways offering work, food, health and childcare, schooling and after-school clubs too. They also do much needed social work by visiting local villages conveying the message as to why it's good and healthy for women to work.

Just holding KnitPro products in your hands shows the other reason why this community engagement is great: the products are manufactured to a very high standard, and are beautiful too. KnitPro also runs a school in a very poor village near New Delhi, providing free education for nearly 900 children.

#socialknitaction

Wood
Flexible and Beautiful.

Akin to metal needles, wooden knitting needles encompass many types of materials: hard and soft woods, rosewood, birch, oak, pine, composites, laminates, ash etc. are all available. Not quite as strong as metal needles, wooden needles are easier on the wrist and hand joints due to the wood flexing slightly to meet the contours and knitting style of the knitter.

The finer the grain of wood and the finer the finish, added with a more satin appearance, leads to increased available speed of use. Wooden needles may need some extra care in terms of oiling or waxing from time to time.

Bamboo
Flexible with a High Friction.

Bamboo: technically a grass not a tree, so not classified with wooden needles. Easy on the hands and flexible, however, the surface friction may be heavy. This may lead to slower stitch formation and movement, but stitches will stay in place longer. Great for knitting with a slippery fibre like silk or viscose as the stitches won't slide about as much on these needles; this also helps with tension in fine projects.

Plastic
Light, Warm and Super Flexible.

Usually brightly coloured, these needles are very easy on the hands and a favourite with arthritis and joint pain sufferers. Stitches can slide easily on plastic needles but they are low in torque for heavy weight projects. This is the type of needle you want if working with very large gauge needles as they are light.

Acrylic
Warm and Light.

More brittle and less flexible than plastic; indeed, with more torque added, acrylic needles may snap. Some though are oh, so pretty.

Carbon
Strong, Light and Warm.

High-tech and stunningly strong; slightly flexible and warm to the touch. As carbon is fibrous, metal tips are usually added to the end to prevent the layers splitting. Easy on the hands, high levels of torque and seriously slick for fast knitting. Ensure the join between the needle tip and carbon shaft is smooth so stitches don't catch when knitting. Only available in one colour. Sex on a stick.

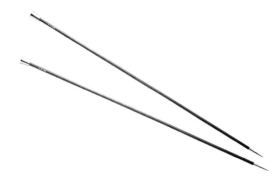

Other Equipment

Best to have a box to keep all items of knitting equipment in and close to hand.

Needle Gauge

A useful item to have in your collection: a plastic or metal item with lots of different sized holes in it to allow you to know what needle size you have.

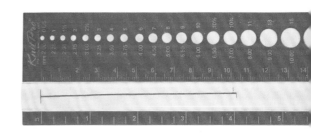

Very useful when converting UK to USA needle sizes or working out the size of a needle if it's displayed in millimetres.

Tape Measure

Fibreglass tape measures that can easily go around the body as well as measuring knitted work are essential. Knitting patterns often state to knit to a certain length, so having a measuring tape to hand is crucial for all projects. Stick to either metric or imperial measurements when knitting, best not to mix them.

Scissors

Small sharp scissors allow for yarn to be cut at the end of a project and to tidy up loose ends when finishing a garment. Using sharp scissors gives a nice clean cut to yarn, reduces snags and yarn unravelling problems.

To prolong the life of your scissors, dedicate a pair solely for knitting. Cutting items like paper or sticky tape will blunt them, resulting in snagged yarn edges.

Row Counter

In our digital age, some things are still best analogue. A little analogue counter that slides onto the end of a needle can be really useful for following patterns, counting rows and stitch routines. These slide onto the end of a knitting needle and are operated by turning the dial on the side to increase or decrease the count as required. It's good to invest in large and small ones so they can fit comfortably onto different size needles.

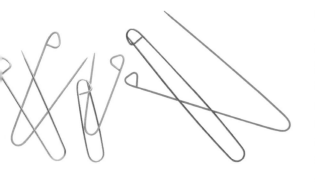

Stitch Holder

When a part of a garment is complete - for example the back of a sweater - some stitches will be left not cast off. These will be used later to knit into the neckband. Once an item is knitted, it is slipped onto a stitch holder so the knitting does not unravel and the stitches don't come undone. If one needs to thread a lot of stitches onto a stitch holder and the stitch holder is too small, the stitches may be threaded onto a length of yarn, ensuring the ends are secured to stop the stitches falling off.

In more advanced knitting projects, stitch holders may be required to hold a part of a knitted line away from the main project for a period of time as per the pattern instructions.

Markers

Little plastic rings can be placed between stitches to show a certain point in a pattern. While knitting, these can be left in the knitted work or moved up to the next row easily as you go. For example: to mark the beginning or end of a round in circular knitting, or to mark a set of counted stitches when knitting or casting on.

I like to place a marker every 50 stitches when doing long cast-ons to help with stitch count.

Other markers, in the form of little clips or trinkets can be clipped directly onto a stitch.

It is also possible to use a piece of yarn as a marker, however, even when in a different colour to the main knitting, it's easy to forget and knit it into the work, forming an extra stitch and that could cause a problem.

Pins

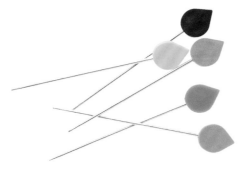

When sewing up the final work and pinning pieces together, it is important to make sure both ends of the work are the same length. As yarn can be a stretchy material, it's important to hold it in place while sewing up. Pins with large brightly coloured heads are available for knitters; they are easier to see than normal pins, which could disappear in the knitting.

Blocking Out Pins

Blocking out is the term used when the finished pieces of knitting are pinned to a board and steamed lightly with a low temperature iron. This allows the fabric to be pressed into shape before sewing up. These pins have large T-shaped heads and are thicker than the pins used to hold fabric together when sewing up. The T-shaped head allows for stitches either side of the pin to be held down securely without snagging.

Sewing Needle and Threader

A wool needle that has a large 'cable eye' is the easiest to both thread and use. Being blunt makes it easier to sew up stitches by guiding the yarn through the stitches, rather than by piercing stitches as would be the case with a sharp needle. It won't hurt either as it won't prick your finger.

Needles with a 'bent tip' are great when sewing up using mattress stitch. It's easier to see the tip when pushing the needle up between stitches.

A needle threader has a bigger eye than the needle and it goes through the eye of the needle easily to make threading simple.

Notebook and Pencil

Always a good idea to have close to hand when knitting to note down stitches or row combinations, sundry jottings, doodles of the finished item, row counts, and much more.

Repair Hook

Repair hooks are small crochet hooks, but double ended with a hook at one end and a point at the other. Available in different sizes, both the hook and point end can be used to repair lost stitches. Really useful when picking up stitches on a neckband or retrieving dropped stitches a few rows back.

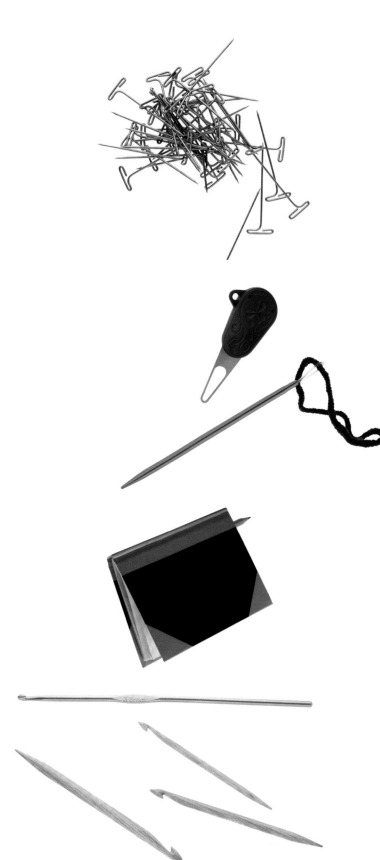

Needle Protectors

Little ends that fit onto the end of knitting needles to stop the points poking through a knitting project bag, and to stop the stitches falling off the ends.

If setting a project down for a week or so, it's advisable to remove the knitting from the needles otherwise a visible line can appear in the finished item. In this case it's best to slide the stitches off the needle onto a length of yarn ensuring the ends are secured.

Ball Holders

Both decorative and practical: either as a bowl, box or spindle, these are great for holding yarn balls while knitting so that they don't roll around. Threading the yarn through the front of the holder also creates a good tension for knitting.

Blocking Mat

A padded board for blocking out items for finishing or for reshaping after washing. One can use an ironing board, however, the pin holes left in the ironing board cover after blocking out are not to everyone's liking. In which case use the KnitPro blocking mats. They are a set of 9 foam mats that can be used individually, or joined together due to their dovetail edges for larger garments.

Ball Winder

A neat way to ensure unravelled balls don't tangle and are not wound too tightly.

Stash Box

Somewhere to store yarn away from sunlight and extremes of temperatures.

Knitting Bags

Somewhere to keep your projects, and yarn too. Bags featured in this book are available from:

knitnibble.com

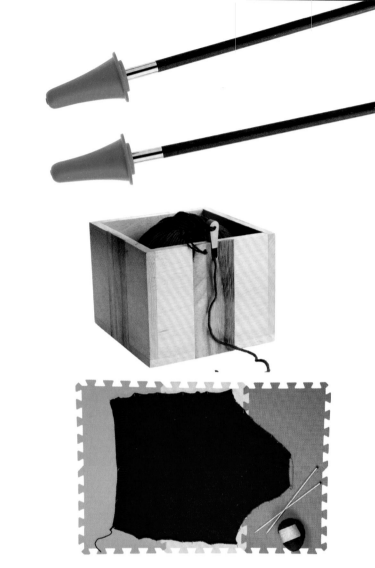

Knitting Tips and Tricks

Some tips and tricks to help you knit better:

- Bigger needles and thicker yarn are easier and quicker to knit than thinner yarn and smaller needles.

- Watch knitting videos online. The internet has lots of videos about knitting. It's a great way to learn new tips and techniques.

- Find a knitting mentor. The gym buddy of knitting. A family member, friend, or from a local knitting group. Knitters are generally very helpful friendly people who will help you if you're struggling with your knitting.

- Keep knitting needles and equipment organised, a box for equipment, a needle case and naturally a yarn box.

- Join a local knitting group. They are everywhere, have a look online and try a few out.

- Knit-as-you-go. Knit on the bus, train, even the plane. Bring your projects with you and knit when you're out of the house and have some downtime.

- Once stitches have been mastered, try memorising patterns. Knitting is just counting, so by memorising your stitch pattern, not only does this improve brain function, it also allows you to knit faster. **#knittitation**

- Always read the pattern before starting. It may look at first a bit overwhelming but, just like cooking a recipe, it's always good to know what's coming next to avoid mistakes.

- Be creative. If you want to change colour, do it. Let the creative you shine.

- When new to knitting, cotton DK is a great beginners choice. Funky yarns, fuzzy, fur, mohair etc. can be too difficult to see stitches on for beginners.

- If you're coming to the end of a ball of yarn and not sure if it will knit another row, just take the yarn tail; as a guide it should be long enough to stretch 4 times across the top of the stitches on the needle.

- Make a habit of counting stitches at the end of each row when you are new to knitting. And then count the row again to double check.

- Always knit a tension square before starting to knit a project. It may seem like extra work and you may want to get straight into your project but you will thank me later for this.

- Like when cooking, best results always come from good quality ingredients. The same is true for knitting. Invest in good quality yarn and needles.

- Blocking out changes a knitted item into a designer item.

- If knitting solely in stocking stitch, the edges will curl up. A few rows of rib at the base and an few alternative stitches on the edges help reduce this.

How to Knit

- Stick the needle through the loop
- Twirl the yarn over
- Push onto other needle
- Repeat

Where Do You Start?

It's actually rather easy. 2 stitches, that's all. One is called **knit**, and the other is called **purl**. Best bit is, neither of them are difficult to do.

Hundreds and thousands of different designs and textures can be created using these 2 stitches in different ways.

Knitting is binary. Instead of 1 and 0 we have **k** and **p**, or knit and purl. It's that easy. And just like binary makes a code, so do stitches or **sts**. Knitting patterns are written in code, but luckily every one in this book comes with abbreviations at the beginning to help you read the pattern.

The 5 steps to making a knitted garment:
1. Cast on
2. Knit
3. Cast off
4. Fix mistakes
5. Sew it together

Knitting is not a race; it's a practice to enjoy at a time and pace that suits you.

It's also important to remember that sometimes in knitting you have to go backwards (rip it out) to go forwards.

Finding the End of your Ball

Before putting the yarn on the needles, the knitter needs to find the end of the ball.

Some may be tempted to remove the ball band on the outside of the yarn to locate the outside edge. Due to the way yarn is spun and the tension of the twisted fibres, it's always best to locate the other end of the yarn by poking your fingers into the middle of the ball and pulling the end out from there. Don't worry if you can't find it straight away; just pull out a little yarn from the middle and follow it to the end.

Using the yarn from the middle of the ball as the starting point will keep the correct twist and tension in the yarn, and stop the ball from flopping about when you're knitting.

How to Hold Knitting Needles

The good news is, there is no right or wrong way, but, some ways are more comfortable than others. If it works for you, do it that way.

- Hold the needles in the palm of your hands

- Don't grip too tight

- Hold the needles near the pointy end (i.e. knit from the top of the needles)

Make a Slip Knot

It's the first thing you need to do: make a loop that won't unravel in the form of a slip knot. Just tying a standard knot will tighten your knitting too much and the finished result won't look so tidy.

- Make a pretzel-shaped loop with the yarn and place one of the knitting needles inside the two smaller holes as like the top of a pretzel.

- Gently pull both lengths of the yarn at the same time to tighten, enough for the yarn to be snug yet still slide up and down the needle comfortably.

This is your first stitch. Now we have to knit some more.

How to Hold the Yarn

Some like to hold the yarn so it's woven through the fingers; others like to run it over the top of a finger that is next to the needle. Like holding the needles, do whatever is comfortable for you. I like to lift the yarn every time I make a stitch, but it's entirely up to you.

When knitting Continental style, yarn is held in the left hand, and when knitting English style, yarn is held in the right hand. Again, it's all down to personal choice.

Casting On

This is the process of making more stitches for the first row of knitting. When the row is complete with the required number of stitches it's known as 'the cast-on edge'. It's from this point that all measurements are taken.

There are various ways to do this. The two needle method is used in this book. It's always easier to get into a rhythm doing this and allow the process to 'flow'. This will come with practise.

Remember that the first cast-on stitch is actually the second stitch, as the slip knot stitch is always counted as the first.

When casting on for a larger project, I always find it easier to work in multiples of 10 or 20, so I place a marker between the stitches. That way it's easier to keep count of how many stitches are on the needle. Once the correct number of stitches have been cast on, recount them to double check.

Take care not to cast on too tightly, or indeed too loosely. The stitches should be able to move with ease when sliding along the knitting needle. Casting on too tightly can cause the first row of knitting to be too tight and as the knitting grows the cast-on edge can look narrower than the main body of the work.

When counting knitted rows, the cast-on row is never counted and is referred to as the 'cast-on edge'.

Have a go using the method below. Rip them out again and keep practising until you can produce a neat row.

Two Needle Cast-on Method:

1. Make a slip knot as described. Have this on the left-hand needle with the tail of the yarn to the back. Have the working yarn to the front of the left-hand needle.

2. Place the tip of the right-hand needle into the slip knot, below the left-hand needle and above the knot itself. Hold in place.

3. Take the working yarn in your right hand and lift it up and over the right-hand needle. The working yarn should now be sitting on top of the right-hand needle with the ball of yarn on your right-hand side.

4. Holding the working yarn gently in your right hand, pull down with the right-hand needle catching the yarn you placed on top of the needle with the yarn and pull through to create a new loop. Place this new loop on the left-hand needle and pull the working yarn to tighten (slightly).

5. Repeat for the required number of stitches.

6. If stuck watch a video online, or ask advice from a knitter you know.

For the Left-Handed Among Us

Knitting patterns are generally (and in this book) written for knitting from the left needle to the right. As knitting is a two-handed activity, the needles can be swapped to the other hands, i.e. knitting from the right to the left. Do whatever feels most comfortable and natural for you, the knitter.

If knitting from right to left, kindly remember you will be looking at the knitted work in reverse, as if a mirror image. So, when it comes to increases and decreases, ensure these are on the other side of your work to what the pattern states.

Knit Stitch

The first row after casting on now needs knitted stitches on top of it to help the project grow. Introducing the knit stitch. It's easy to do, and with time and practise a rather speedy stitch to complete.

1. Hold the needle with the cast on stitches in your left hand with the ball of working yarn to your right.

2. With the empty needle in your right hand, place the tip of the right-hand needle to the left of the first stitch.

3. Slide the right-hand needle under the stitch at the end of the left-hand needle between the left-hand needle and the top of the cast-on row.

4. Poke the right-hand needle out slightly, pushing away from the left-hand needle and wrap your working yarn over the top of the right-hand needle.

5. Pull the yarn placed over the right-hand needle through the bottom of the left-hand needle in a gentle motion gliding off the left-hand needle onto the right-hand needle.

6. Continue as above for all stitches on the left-hand needle.

N.B.

The first row of stitches after casting on may appear slightly tight. If too tight, rip out and cast on again a little looser. As you knit more rows your tension should regulate.

Once this knit row is finished, turn the knitting round (the wrong side of the knitting will now be facing you) and learn how to purl the next row.

Purl Stitch

Knit as for the knit stitch, but instead of going from the left of the stitch, go from the right.

Knowing Your Garters From Your Stockings

Rows of just a knit stitch result in a bumpy finish called garter stitch.

Alternative rows of knit one row and purl the next result in a smooth finish called stocking stitch.

After mastering these 2 basic stitches, a few others - equally as easy - are used in this book:

Rib

As the name suggests, ribbed knitting looks corrugated. Used in different sizes, e.g. 1x1 rib, 2x2 rib or 4x2 rib, it produces a mixture of mountains and valleys in the final knitted work. A rib is more than an effect: it keeps knitting from rolling up at the end and provides strength to knitted edges. It is a mixture of knit one stitch and purl the next in the case of a 1x1 rib or knit 2 stitches and purl the next 2 in the case of a 2x2 rib and so on.

Through the Back Loop

When knitting, one knits through the loop at the front of the needle facing you, until this cheeky little stitch (either knit or purl as directed by the pattern) appears. Through the back loop is easy: just knit or purl as directed through the other side of the stitch on the needle; known as the back loop.

Knit One Below

In the *Pour* pattern, page 142, you will find this stitch in the pattern. Simply knit into the hole at the top of the stitch below rather than into the stitch on the needle. This results in a stitch that is bumpy in texture.

Knit Two / Three Together

Simply put, knit two / three stitches into one.

Purl Two / Three Together

The same as above only using the purl stitch rather than the knit stitch.

Make One Stitch

When increasing stitches in a pattern, sometimes the pattern will state to make one stitch. This is done by knitting into the front and back of the first or last stitch in a row (as directed by the pattern) to make two stitches.

Slip One, Knit One, Pass the Slipped Stitch Over

As it says, move one stitch from the left-hand needle to the right without knitting or purling. Knit one stitch and then place the first stitch that you slipped onto the right-hand needle and over the second stitch, allowing it to fall off.

Casting Off

When the knitting is at the correct length you will need to cast off. This is easy to do. Working on the right side of the work, knit the first two stitches, lift the first stitch over the second and let it drop off the right-hand needle. Continue along the left-hand needle (always with one stitch on the right-hand needle) until all stitches are off the needle. Leave a tail, cut the yarn and pull through the last stitch to secure.

Cast Off Variants

Some patterns state to cast off in rib. This is the same as casting off normally, only you knit one stitch, purl the next, lift the knit stitch over the purl stitch and drop the knit stitch off the needle, and then knit another and drop the purl stitch. I assure you it's easier to do than read.

One can cast off on a purl row or what is called 'in pattern'. Just follow the directions in the knitting patterns in this book and remember to lift one stitch over the previously worked stitch to cast off.

Pick Up Stitches

This is required when working neckbands on cast-off pieces of work. Just lift the stitch using a hook onto a needle from the finished work for the required number at the required intervals as dictated by the knitting pattern.

28 rows

22 sts

Tension

Everyone knits at a slightly different tension; some may be too tight and some may be too loose. As a guide, to make sure your knitting matches that of the pattern, knit a swatch, which is called a *tension square*.

What's the Correct Tension?

Every ball of yarn will have the tension and the size of needles required to knit to that tension on the label. This is known as the *gauge* in knitting. All tension squares should be 10 x 10cm (4 x 4in) when completed with the stated size needles in the knitting pattern and on the yarn ball label. Thicker yarn requires larger needles and thinner yarn requires smaller needles.

Double Knitting Tension

For Sirdar Double Knitting (DK) yarns this equates to 22 stitches knit in stocking stitch (knit one row and purl the next, repeat) for 28 rows on 4mm needles..

In turn, this also tells you how many stitches to cast on for other projects: by dividing 10 by 22 = 2.2 stitches per cm required for the width; by dividing 10 by 28 = 2.8 stitches per cm for the height.

If your knitting turns out to be less than 10 x 10cm (4 x 4in) try and knit the square again using knitting needles a size bigger, or a size smaller if your tension square is larger.

Making a tension square is a good way to check colour combinations and stitch patterns too. It also gives you a safe laundry test sample. Many knitters save their tension squares to make blankets and cushion covers.

Congratulations, you have now knitted your first project.

Tension square in Sublime Extra Fine Merino DK

22 stitches x 28 rows in stocking stitch = 10cm (4in) square.

This tension square has been surrounded in garter stitch.

New Balls Please

It takes more yarn to knit a row than you may think. Whether it's changing colour, or just knitting to the end of the ball, most knitting projects will require adding a new ball of yarn at various points as the knitting grows.

It's always neatest to work to the end of the row and then knit with a new ball of yarn, pulling the tails gently after a few stitches, which helps maintain tension. No need to tie a knot when adding a new ball.

I find it best to leave a tail of about 10cm (4in) at each end for sewing in neatly at the end of the project.

Adding a new ball of yarn midway through a row will leave a little bump in the knitted item, so take the time and rip the row back.

Sometimes you may find a very tight little knot in the yarn. This is simply due to the spinning process and it's best to ensure this knot is at the end of the knitted project. Sadly, and I sympathise with your demonised enthusiasm here, you may have to rip back the row you have just knit.

Save remnants of yarn ends for sewing up later.

Which Way is Which?

Knitted work has a right side and a wrong side.

The right side is the outside side or front of the finished work and the wrong side is the back of the work. The wrong side of a jumper therefore is the inside.

It's easy to confuse the right and wrong side with the right-hand and left-hand side of the body, so in knitting patterns the terms **RS** for right side of the work, and **WS** for the wrong side of the work are used.

The right side of the work is easy to see. Go back to the cast-on edge (if having cast on with two needles as described in this book) and if the tail of the yarn is on the left and the needle is pointing to the right, this is the **RS**

of the work. If the tail of the cast-on edge is on the right and the needle is pointing to the right, then this is the **WS** of the work.

How to Tell a Knit Stitch or Row

If you're on a Right Side row and the tail from casting on is to the left, and the point of the needle is to the right (with right side facing up), whatever is facing you, as you look at it, is what you do. And, the working yarn is coming out of the back of the stitch.

When flipped over, the point of the needle pointing to the left, the working yarn is to the back of the knitting, and the last row has 'bumps' on the back at each stitch, then the last row knitted would be a purl row.

If 'bumps' appear on the front row after knitting, just below the needle, and you are knitting in stocking stitch, then rip out, recount the stitches on the needle to ensure they are correct and purl rather than knit.

If the yarn is coming out of the back of the stitch, the last stitch was a knit stitch. If the yarn is coming out of the front of the stitch, the last stich was a purl stitch.

How to Tell a Purl Stitch or Row

If you're on a Right Side row and the tail from casting on is to the right, and the point of the needle is to the right (with right side facing up), whatever is facing you, as you look at it, is what you do. And, the working yarn is coming out of the back of the stitch.

When flipped over, with the point of the needle pointing to the left and the working yarn is to the back of the knitting, and the last row has 'bumps' on the back at each stitch, then the last row knitted would be a purl row.

If 'bumps' appear on the front row after knitting and you are knitting in stocking stitch, then rip out, recount the stitches on the needle to ensure they are correct and knit rather than purl.

If the yarn is coming out of the front of the previous stitch, the last stitch was a purl stitch.

Counting Stitches

Counting stitches is a great habit to get into. A pattern requires a set amount of stitches for both the design of the finished item and for the production of the correctly sized work. When stitches are on one needle, it's a simple matter of counting the stitches in that row along the top of the needle.

If there are a lot of stitches, it can be easy to miscount, so why not count to 20, place a marker at that point and then start at number 1 again until the next number 20. Then count the 20s.

Don't forget to count the initial slip knot as stitch 1 if counting the cast-on row.

Counting Rows

Counting rows is a little trickier than counting stitches, especially for the novice knitter. However, here are my top tips to help you:

1. Place a marker at the top of the row you have chosen to count.
2. Pull the knitted work slightly in both directions and count the bars in the middle of the stitches.
3. Never count the cast-on row.
4. Always include the row of stitches on the needle.
5. To avoid having to do this, keep a row counter uptodate while knitting.
6. Measure the height of the work and calculate using the number of rows from the gauge worked out in the tension square, page 49.

Need a Break?

When stopping knitting for a break, always finish the row you're working on and adjust the row counter if necessary. Doing this prevents stretched stitches in the middle of a row.

If you're going to leave a knitting project for a period of time, it's best to thread some yarn (in a different colour) through the stitches and remove the needle. Leaving them on the needle can stretch the stitches resulting in an unwelcome line in the finished garment. Ensure both ends of the contrast yarn are tied together so the stitches don't fall off. When ready to start knitting again, simply slide the stitches back onto a needle and carry on knitting.

Abbreviation	Meaning
c	contrast colour
cm	centimetre(s)
DK	double knitting
g	gramm(es)
in	inch(es)
k	knit
m	main colour
mm	millimetres
St(s)	stitch(es)
p	purl
ws	wrong side
rs	right side
0	no stitches, times or rows
tog	together
k2tog / k3tog	knit 2/3 stitches together
k1below	knit 1 stitch into the stitch below
patt	pattern
p2tog	purl 2 stitches together
p2togtbl	purl 2 stitches together through the back loop
s1	slip 1 stitch
psso	pass the slipped stitch over
m1	make 1 stitch, by kniting into both the front and the back of one stitch to make 2 stitches
tbl	through the back loop
*****	the start and end of a sequence (more than one * may be present depending on pattern)
[ ]	differentiation of different sizes
rib2tog	knit 2 rib stitches together
patt2tog	knit 2 stitches together as for the stitch pattern in the pattern instructions

KNIT 1, NIBBLE 1

K1, N1

REPEAT FROM *TO*

Reading a Knitting Pattern

Terminology

Let's be honest, at first glance knitting patterns look like they are full of tosh.

Grab a cuppa. Let me explain. I call it **KnitM^cIntosh**.

KnitM^cIntosh *noun*

"A combination of the knitting language and the concept of 'a load of old Tosh',

as named by James McIntosh MA."

These abbreviations are consistent with any knitting pattern written in the English language and are simply a combination of asterisks, parentheses, numbers and other shorthand spellings. The reality is, if a complete knitting pattern was written out in full, it would take up pages and pages.

The table opposite translates KnitM^cIntosh for the items in this book.

Also note: square brackets are used in patterns to determine larger sizes of garments.

E.g. the smallest size is always in **BLUE** and outside of the square brackets, followed by [**ORANGE**, **GREEN**, **BLACK**, YELLOW and PINK] inside square brackets in size order as outlined on page 20.

Both beginner and experienced knitters can write out the patterns in longer form as they knit. This can be useful when increasing or decreasing a sleeve for example. Personally, I like to write down all of the row numbers and write next to the corresponding row if I need to increase or decrease stitches and by how many, ticking off as I go. Others may use a row counter and just write out the row numbers where the increases or decreases occur, remembering to add a new number to the row counter as they go.

Final Techniques and Tricks

Capital Letters: knitting patterns are written in 'sentence case', so there is no difference between a **K** for knit and a **k** for knit, for example. It all depends if it is at the beginning of a sentence or not.

Fasten Off: pull the yarn through the last stitch(es) as directed by the pattern and leave a long tail.

At the Same Time: this notation in a pattern can lead to horrible results if not read correctly. Basically, it's a time to prove that you can multitask. A good example is when decreasing for an armhole at the top of the front of a jumper when decreasing also needs to be carried out **at the same time** for the neckline.

Back of Your Work: this is the knitted work you have created that is not facing you as you knit. Don't confuse it with the right side **rs** and wrong side **ws** of the knitting, which is the description of how the knitted item will be sewn up for wearing.

Cast Off from Each Neck Edge: when shaping a neck, both sides are decreased at the same time in some items, but one shapes the right side (as worn) on right side **rs** rows and the wrong side (as worn) on wrong side **ws** rows. It may sound complicated, but when knitting, it's rather instinctive.

Cast Off in Patt: cast off following the stitch requirement as per the pattern of previous row.

End After a Wrong Side Row: simply put, if you are knitting, the last side of this part of the pattern knit should be a wrong side **ws**, meaning, the next row to be knit should be the right side **rs**.

Increase or Decrease Every 4 Rows: this is a classic term when knitting a sleeve. In this example (usually on the right side of the work) one would increase by using the **m1** (make one stitch) at each end (or as stated by pattern) in row 1 and then rows 5, 9, 13, 17 etc., or decrease by using the **k2tog** (knit 2 stitches together). The rows in the middle are knit as normal with no increases or decreases: rows 2, 3 and 4 are knit normally as per pattern.

45 Stitches on Your Needle: it's really important to have the correct number of stitches (**sts**) on your needle at set points when knitting a project as determined by the pattern (**patt**). Always check the stitch count as stated in the pattern at certain points.

Increase or Decrease Every Other Row: simply put, follow the pattern to either increase or decrease on one row and then knit or purl the next row as per the pattern.

Place Marker: use a plastic ring, piece of yarn (in a different colour) or a safety pin to mark a place in the knitting. This is useful for matching different pieces (e.g. sleeve decreasing) when sewing up.

Right: as the knitting would be worn on the body. Hold the knitting against the body and note the right side **ws** of the work against the right-hand side of the body.

Left: as the knitting would be worn on the body. Hold the knitting against the body and note the right side **ws** of the work against the left-hand side of the body.

Armhole Measurements: knit as per pattern until a set measurement, remembering to measure a straight line, not around the shape of the armhole.

Work as For: referred to knitting the front of a jumper and marked in a pattern by a set of asterisks **. Patterns in this book are written for knitting jumpers in the following order:

- Back
- Front
- Sleeves x 2
- Neckband

Work to End: knit to the end of the row using the same stitch pattern.

Continue In ...: as outlined in the pattern, the name of a stitch pattern defined earlier in the pattern.

Continue to Length Required: some people may require a longer sleeve than others or have a larger torso, thereby requiring a few more rows of stitches. Continue knitting as per the previous rows without decreasing or increasing to continue to pattern to the required length. This is easily worked out by using the gauge from a tension square on page 49 to determine how many extra rows are required.

Definitions: definitions for all abbreviations used in a pattern are outlined at the beginning.

Divide for Neck and Turn: a neck is knit in two parts. Knit up to the beginning of the neck, place the required number of stitches onto a stitch holder and knit one side of the neck. When complete, return (some or all - see pattern) the stitches on the stitch holder onto the knitting needle, and knit the other side as instructed in the pattern.

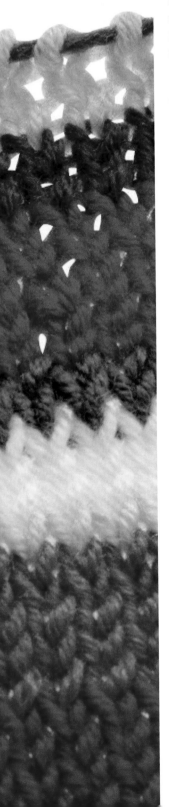

Draw Up: pull the yarn (that has been cut) through the stitch(es).

Every Following Alternate Row: used when a stitch pattern or increasing/decreasing is involved. Follow the pattern changes in the row after next, and then the row after that. E.g.: row 2, 4, 6, 8 etc. Other rows should be knit as the pattern stated previously.

Every Following 4th Row: as for every following alternate row above, but the changes in the pattern are every following 4th (or number stated) rather than every other row.

Patt to End: follow the pattern guidelines to the end of the row.

Run Yarn Through Remaining Sts: using a tapestry needle, pull the yarn through the stitch(es).

These 2 Rows Form: the name of a stitch pattern created by knitting the previous 2 rows (or however many rows stated).

Work in A / B / C etc: indicating a change in colour; colours are laid out at the beginning of the pattern. This term is used when there are more than 2 colour choices. In this instance **m** and **c** are used (main and contrast) colours.

Turn: turn the knitting needle with the yarn and knitting in the same position. This is required when working on neckline decreases.

Special Characters to Make Life Easier

Asterisk

An indication that a set of instructions should be repeated. A set of one, two, or more asterisks will be present in the pattern, clearly indicating what to do 1st as in first, second etc.; not to be confused with 1 stitch (1st).

Commas

Single steps in a pattern are separated by commas. Follow the pattern to the comma, and see this as one step, then breathe, and move onto the next step.

Curved Brackets

An indication of how many repeats of a dedicated stitch pattern are required. Eg:

Knit McIntosh: *K5, (p1, K2) twice, p1; repeat from * to end of row.

Longhand: knit 5 stitches, purl 1 stitch, knit the next 2 stitches, purl 1 stitch, knit the next 2 stitches, purl 1 stitch and repeat the whole of this sequence until the end of the row.

Square Brackets

Indicates the numbers required for different sizes of items.

Measuring Knitted Work

A knitting pattern will give measurements, e.g.:

- Knit for 5 rows
- Knit in pattern for 4 rows or
- Knit until work measures 46cm from cast-on edge

Knitting a set number of rows is easy by recording the row count using either a row counter or a tally mark on a piece of paper.

To knit to a certain size, knit to the middle of your work so the knitting spreads across both needles, lie the knitted work flat on a table and measure from the centre to the cast-on edge. Make sure there are no bumps in your work as these will increase the length.

It's always easier to use a flat tape measure and measure from the bottom up. Read the measurement from the top of the needle; the stitches on the needle would form the cast-off edge if this was the end of the project, thereby giving the correct height of the finished item.

Getting measurements incorrect or knitting short will result in short sleeves for example, and nobody wants that do they?

If measuring an armhole, or other curved item, always measure straight up, i.e. from the start of the decreasing in a straight line to the top. Finally, never measure around the curve.

I'M A KNOTTY KNOTTY KNITTER

Lifeline

When knitting, sometimes one needs to go back to go forward, commonly known as 'ripping out'. A lifeline is a line of sewn yarn (often in a different colour so it's visible) that's quick to sew in and allows for ripping back the knitting to a particular row allowing you to pick up from there and go forward again. Panic and fear can hit the knitter about ripping out work, but this easy method will hold everything in place. Plus, the stitches held together by the lifeline are easy to put back onto the needle.

Thread a needle with some waste yarn - longer than the knitted item is wide. Pass the needle carrying the yarn through the right hand side of each stitch (if working in stocking stitch) from left to right, going through each stitch in the row. When you rip back to this point, the loops of the knitting that would sit on a needle are held on the lifeline.

Alternatively, sew from left to right through each stitch on the knitting needle. Knit the next row to allow for a marker in the knitting. To remove the lifeline, simply pull it out.

Time to Put it all Together

An item is knit, it's time to put it all together. Before sewing, it's best to 'block it out'. This not only allows the finished garment to look neater, but allows for easier sewing up.

Using blocking mats and pins, place the knitted item wrong side up. Pin out to the measurements given in the pattern and with a steam iron (on a low temperature) steam the item. This plumps up the fibres and straightens out the edges. All patterns in this book that require sewing up have 2 extra stitches written into the pattern, one at each end. These are what one sews up, so it's important to steam right to the very edge of the item.

After steaming, leave to dry naturally. Remove from the board and sew up.

Sewing it Up

Sewing up is rather easy. It comes in two parts:

1. Sew up the seams using mattress stitch
2. Sew in the ends

To sew up the seam, lay the knitted garment flat and pin out using large marking pins ensuring the right side of the garment is facing you. Sew large tacking stitches in a different colour of yarn to make it all hold together.

Thread a needle with a long length of yarn. Secure yarn on the back of the right-hand knitted piece.

From the back, bring the needle up between the first and second stitches immediately above the cast-on edge. Take it across to the left-hand piece, and from the back bring it through between the first and second stitches of the piece immediately above the cast-on edge. Take it back to the right-hand piece and again from the back, bring it through one row above where it first came through, between the first and second stitches. Pull yarn through - this will hold the cast-on edges level.

Take the needle across to the left-hand piece, from the front, under the 'bar' of yarn above where it last came out on the side between first and second stitches.

Take the needle across to the right-hand piece and from the front, take it under the next 2 bars of yarn between the first and second stitch. Pull through. Take the needle back to the left-hand piece and from the front, under the corresponding two bars between the first and second stitches. Repeat until all knitted edges are sewn together. There should be a little 'rib' on the wrong side of the work and be flat on the right side of the knitted work.

Sew in leftover ends by threading the yarn tail onto a needle. Weave the needle up and down through the backs (wrong side) of 3 or 4 stitches that are the same colour as the yarn.

Weave the needle back through the stitches in the opposite direction and cut off excess yarn.

Garment Care

Taking Your Clothes Off

It's so tempting for some to grab a jumper by the neck and pull it over the head. This may result in a stretched yoke at the back and it won't look so good when next worn. For best practice, always grab either side of the bottom of the jumper (the welt) and pull upwards, over the head and down the sleeves. Then simply turn the other way round to have the right side facing.

Laundering

When knit in Sirdar or Sublime yarn, a knitted product will keep for many years if it's laundered correctly. It's a good idea to keep the yarn ball band so you can always refer to the washing instructions in future. For best results, wash as soon as a stain appears and if there is more than one type of Sirdar or Sublime yarn in a project, always use the lesser of the wash care settings.

Swatch Test

If you're unsure how best to wash a garment, it's easy to do a little test with the tension square knitted before starting a project. Wash this on its own as you intend to wash the whole garment, allow to dry and ensure it comes out the same size as it went in, and without a felted appearance.

Machine Washing

For any machine washable items use a low temperature. 30°C is a good temperature to wash knitted items using a washing machine wool cycle. Any hotter and the fibres in the yarn may lock together and the item will shrink.

Hand Washing

Using cool water (not cold), wash the item gently and wash one garment at a time. Don't twist or rub the fabric and wash as quickly and as gently as possible. It's important to rinse the garment well, ensuring the water has run clear indicating that all of the soap has been removed.

Detergents

Gentle wool wash detergents are available for both machine and hand washing. Avoid any detergents containing optical brighteners.

Drying

Place the garment on a towel and roll it up, which should absorb most of the moisture. Never ring or squeeze to remove the water, this may misshapen the garment. Likewise, hanging a knitted garment to dry will stretch it, so best to dry flat on a clean towel. If it's a little misshapen, pin it out to shape with blocking pins as noted on page 39. Dry away from any heat source or direct sunlight and change the towel underneath every few hours.

Stain Removal

Stains are either the result of an accident or a good night out!

Always soak the garment in cold water (never hot) to remove the stain. Don't rub or it could stretch the knitting, resulting in a misshapen garment. If the stain does not come out, use a commercial stain remover.

Storage

Folded neatly, knitted items can be stored on a wardrobe shelf or in a drawer. Always best to store flat and not on hangers, away from direct sunlight and thoroughly dried beforehand.

Moths

Moths love wool. They lay their eggs in wool and when hatched wool provides an endless supply of lovely meals for the little darlings. Holes appear in knitting and darning is required in to mend. Pleasant smelling cedar wood balls are cheap to purchase from a hardware store. To get rid of the little blighters, store knitted items with cedar balls.

If moths nibble a knitted item, it's always sensible to keep a little of the yarn used to knit the project to hand, for mending any holes. Buying new yarn at this stage may result in colour issues due to the yarn's dye lot.

Gentle machine wash at 30°C

Can be dry cleaned

Do not iron

Do not tumble dry

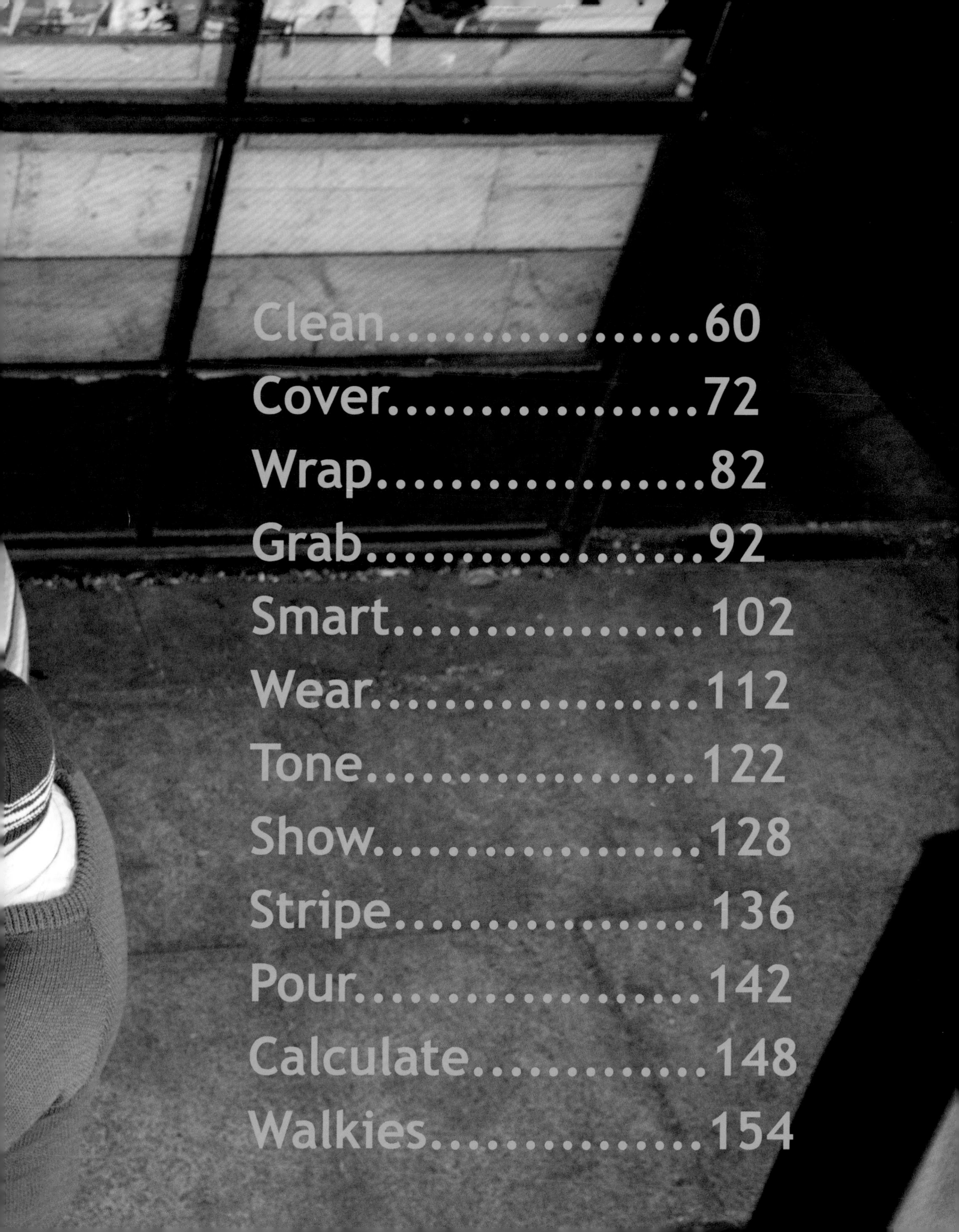

Clean.

Yourself. Kitchen. Bathroom. Car.

To learn to knit, one has to make mistakes.

In knitting beginners need to rip out to go forward.

Reversing to go the right way.

Sort of like learning to control the break and clutch when learning to drive a manual car.

Never mind following a pattern, it's the navigation system.

Learn to knit by making a cloth.

The finished product may have mistakes in it, but the pots and pans won't mind.

And practice makes perfect.

Knit in Sirdar Cotton DK in a choice of 210 colour combinations.

- Garter Stitch Cloth
- Stocking Stitch Cloth
- 1x1 Rib Cloth
- 2x2 Rib Cloth
- 4x2 Rib Cloth

Clean - let's make some stitches.

Garter Stitch Cloth.

Just knit rows for garter stitch - the easiest and quickest of all patterns to knit.

Makes 1 x Garter Stitch Cloth in Sirdar Cotton DK
Width x Length (approximately) 24 x 24cm (9½ x 9½in)

1 x 100g ball Sirdar Cotton DK shade **501 - Mill White** for main colour

1 x oddment Sirdar Cotton DK shade **511 - Hot Pink** for contrast colour

1 x pair 4mm knitting needles (or the size required to give the correct tension)

1 x notepad and pen

1 x measuring tape

1 x scissors

1 x sewing needle

Abbreviations

cm centimetres, **C** contrast, **DK** double knitting, **g** grammes, **in** inch(es), **k** knit, **M** main, **mm** millimetres, **st(s)** stitch(es), **ws** wrong side.

Here's how to make it ...

Check one's tension

With clean hands, cast on **21 sts** and knit **38 rows** in garter stitch (knit each row) on **4mm** needles or the size required to give correct tension, which should result in a **10cm (4in)** square.

If the square is bigger than this, use a thinner needle, if smaller use a thicker needle.

It's really important to get this bit correct or the cloth will not result in the sizes stated.

Cast on

Using C, cast on 50 sts.

Change colour

Change to M and continue as follows:

> **1ˢᵗ Row** (this will be the right side of the work - **rs**). Knit.

This row forms garter stitch.

Knit the cloth

Work in garter stitch until cloth measures 24cm, (9 ½in), finishing after a ws row.

Change colour

Change to C and work 1 row more.

Cast off

Cast off knitways.

To serve

Lather with soapy water and use as required.

See yarn ball band for washing and further care instructions.

Something to clean, kitchen perhaps?

If made up after 6pm, serve as above, take picture and post to social media with choice of cleaning product in hand.

#knitandnibble #clean #imadethis

Stocking Stitch Cloth.

Just knit one row using a knit stitch, and the next row with a purl stitch.
Just like going backwards and forwards.

Makes 1 x Stocking Stitch Cloth in Sirdar Cotton DK.
Width x Length (approximately) 23 x 23cm (9 x 9in)

1 x 100g ball Sirdar Cotton DK shade **501 - Mill White** for main colour

1 x oddment Sirdar Cotton DK shade **514 - French Navy** for contrast colour

1 x pair 4mm knitting needles (or the size required to give the correct tension)

1 x notepad and pen

1 x measuring tape

1 x scissors

1 x sewing needle

Abbreviations

cm centimetres, **C** contrast, **DK** double knitting, **g** grammes, **in** inch(es), **k** knit, **M** main, **mm** millimetres, **st(s)** stitch(es).

Here's how to make it ...

Check one's tension

With clean hands, cast on **22 sts** and knit **28 rows** in garter stitch (knit each row) on **4mm** needles or the size required to give correct tension, which should result in a **10cm (4in)** square.

If the square is bigger than this, use a thinner needle, if smaller use a thicker needle.

It's really important to get this bit correct or the cloth will not result in the sizes stated.

Cast on

Using C, cast on 50 sts.

Change colour

Change to M and continue as follows:

    1st Row. Knit.
    2nd Row. Purl.

These 2 rows form stocking stitch.

Knit the cloth

Work in stocking stitch until cloth measures 23cm, (9in), finishing after a knit row.

Change colour

Change to C and purl to end.

Cast off

Cast off knitways.

To serve

Lather with soapy water and use as required.

See yarn ball band for washing and further care instructions.

Something to clean. You perhaps?

If made up after 6pm, serve as above, take picture and post to social media with choice of soap in hand.

#knitandnibble #clean #imadethis

1x1 Rib Cloth.

Just knit one stitch using a knit stitch, and purl next stitch.
Moving the yarn from front to back is like sitting on a see-saw.

Makes 1 x 1x1 Rib Cloth in Sirdar Cotton DK
Width x Length (approximately) 23 x 23cm (9 x 9in)

1 x 100g ball Sirdar Cotton DK shade **501 - Mill White** for main colour

1 x oddment Sirdar Cotton DK shade **512 - Black Violet** for contrast colour

1 x pair 3.5mm knitting needles (or the size required to give the correct tension)

1 x notepad and pen

1 x measuring tape

1 x scissors

1 x sewing needle

Abbreviations

cm centimetres, **C** contrast, **DK** double knitting, **g** grammes, **in** inch(es), **k** knit, **M** main, **mm** millimetres, **p** purl, **rs** right side, **st(s)** stitch(es).

Here's how to make it ...

Check one's tension

With clean hands, cast on **26 sts** and knit **30 rows** in 1x1 rib when stretched to correct width on **3.5mm** needles or the size required to give correct tension, which should result in a **10cm (4in)** square.

If the square is bigger than this, use a thinner needle, if smaller use a thicker needle.

It's really important to get this bit correct or the cloth will not result in the sizes stated.

Cast on

Using C, cast on 61 sts.

Change colour

Change to M and continue as follows:

   1ˢᵗ Row. * K1, p1, repeat from * to last st, k1.
   2ⁿᵈ Row. P1, * k1, p1, repeat from * to end.

These 2 rows form 1x1 rib.

Knit the cloth

Work in 1x1 rib until cloth measures 23cm, (9in), finishing after a rs row.

Change colour

Change to C and rib to end.

Cast off

Cast off in rib.

To serve

Lather with soapy water and use as required.

See yarn ball band for washing and further care instructions.

Something to clean. Car?

If made up after 6pm, serve as above, take picture and post to social media with picture of car in background.

#knitandnibble #clean #imadethis

2x2 Rib Cloth.

Just knit two stitches using a knit stitch, and purl the next two stitches. Making a deeper groove than the 1x1 rib.

Makes 1 x 2x2 Rib Cloth in Sirdar Cotton DK.
Width x Length (approximately) 24 x 24cm (9 ½ x 9 ½in)

1 x 100g ball Sirdar Cotton DK shade **501 - Mill White** for main colour

1 x oddment Sirdar Cotton DK shade **510 - Galore Red** for contrast colour

1 x pair 3.5mm knitting needles (or the size required to give the correct tension)

1 x notepad and pen

1 x measuring tape

1 x scissors

1 x sewing needle

Abbreviations

cm centimetres, **C** contrast, **DK** double knitting, **g** grammes, **in** inch(es), **k** knit, **M** main, **mm** millimetres, **p** purl, **rs** right side, **st(s)** stitch(es).

Here's how to make it ...

Check one's tension

With clean hands, cast on **26 sts** and knit **30 rows** in 2x2 rib when stretched to correct width on **3.5mm** needles or the size required to give correct tension, which should result in a **10cm (4in)** square.

If the square is bigger than this, use a thinner needle, if smaller use a thicker needle.

It's really important to get this bit correct or the cloth will not result in the sizes stated.

Cast on

Using C, cast on 62 sts.

Change colour

Change to M and continue as follows:

    1ˢᵗ Row. * K2, p2, repeat from * to last 2 sts, k2.
    2ⁿᵈ Row. P2, * k2, p2, repeat from * to end.

These 2 rows form 2x2 rib.

Knit the cloth

Work in 2x2 rib until cloth measures 24cm, (9 ½in), finishing after a rs row.

Change colour

Change to C and rib to end.

Cast off

Cast off in rib.

To serve

Lather with soapy water and use as required.

See yarn ball band for washing and further care instructions.

Something to clean. Bathroom?

If made up after 6pm, serve as above, take picture and post to social media with rubber duck in shot.

#knitandnibble #clean #imadethis

4x2 Rib Cloth.

Just knit four stitches using a knit stitch, and purl the next two stitches, making a deeper wave and a groove as with the 2x2 rib.

Makes 1 x 4x2 Rib Cloth in Sirdar Cotton DK.
Width x Length (approximately) 24 x 24cm (9 ½ x 9 ½in)

1 x 100g ball Sirdar Cotton DK shade **501 - Mill White** for main colour

1 x oddment Sirdar Cotton DK shade **515 - Bluebird** for contrast colour

1 x pair 3.5mm knitting needles (or the size required to give the correct tension)

1 x notepad and pen

1 x measuring tape

1 x scissors

1 x sewing needle

Abbreviations

cm centimetres,**C** contrast, **DK** double knitting, **g** grammes, **in** inch(es), **k** knit, **M** main, **mm** millimetres, **p** purl, **rs** right side, **st(s)** stitch(es).

Here's how to make it ...

Check one's tension

With clean hands, cast on **24 sts** and knit **30 rows** in 4x2 rib when stretched to correct width on **3.5mm** needles or the size required to give correct tension, which should result in a **10cm (4in)** square.

If the square is bigger than this, use a thinner needle, if smaller use a thicker needle.

It's really important to get this bit correct or the cloth will not result in the sizes stated.

Cast on

Using C, cast on 58 sts.

Change colour

Change to M and continue as follows:

    1ˢᵗ Row. K4, * p2, k4, repeat from * to end.
    2ⁿᵈ Row. * P4, * k2, repeat from * to last 4 sts, p4.

These 2 rows form 4x2 rib.

Knit the cloth

Work in 4x2 rib until cloth measures 24cm, (9 ½in), finishing after a rs row.

Change colour

Change to C and rib to end.

Cast off

Cast off in rib.

To serve

See yarn ball band for washing and further care instructions.

Something to clean. Computer?

If made up after 6pm, serve as above, take picture and post to social media.

Cover.

Some things look better covered. Fact.
Practising knitting helps to build confidence
Colours your life
Keeps your beer can cool
Covers a wine bottle for a wine tasting
Polishes and protects a phone or hip flask

Knit in Sublime Extra Fine Merino DK,

each cover in a choice of 465 colour combinations.

- Phone Cover
- Swig Hip Flask Cover
- Beer Can Cover
- Wine Bottle Cover

Cover - learning how to sew up.

Sublime
extra fine merino wool dk

Phone Cover.

Polish the screen as you go.
A new variant on 'whistle while you work'.

Makes 1 x mobile phone cover in Sublime Extra Fine Merino DK.
Width x Length (approximately) 14 x 12cm (5 ½ x 4 ¾in)

1 x 50g ball Sublime Extra Fine Merino DK shade **363 - Indigo** for main colour

1 x 50g ball Sublime Extra Fine Merino DK shade **577 - Parisian Sky** for contrast colour

1 x pair 3.5mm knitting needles (or the size required to give the correct tension)

1 x notepad and pen

1 x measuring tape

1 x scissors

1 x sewing needle

Abbreviations

cm centimetres, **C** contrast, **DK** double knitting, **g** grammes, **in** inch(es), **k** knit, **M** main, **mm** millimetres, **p** purl, **st(s)** stitch(es).

Here's how to make it ...

Check one's tension

With clean hands, cast on **26 sts** and knit **30 rows** on **3.5mm** needles or the size required to give correct tension, which should result in a **10cm (4in)** square.

If the square is bigger than this, use a thinner needle, if smaller use a thicker needle.

It's really important to get this bit correct or the phone cover will not result in the sizes stated.

Cast on

Measure the circumference of the phone in cm, multiply the measurement by 2.6 to find number of cast on sts ensuring an odd number. Eg, 16cm x 2.6 = 41.6 = 41 sts. Using M, cast on number required sts.

Knit the body

1st **Row.** * K1, p1; repeat from * to last st, k1.
2nd **Row.** P1, * k1, p1, repeat from * to end.
These 2 rows form 1x1 rib.

Work in 1x1 rib until cover is half the height of phone.

Change colour

Change to C and work in 1x1 rib until cover is ¾ height of phone.

Cast off

Cast off in rib.

To serve

Fold cover in half lengthways, join side and lower edge seams.

See yarn ball band for washing and further care instructions.

Insert phone.

#knitandnibble #cover #imadethis

Swig Hip Flask Cover.

Protect your Swig® hip flask.
swigflasks.com

Swig®

Makes 1 x Swig hip flask cover in Sublime Extra Fine Merino DK
Width x Length (approximately) 20.5 x 8cm (8 ¼ x 3in)

1 x 50g ball Sublime Extra Fine Merino DK shade **017 - Redcurrant** for main colour

1 x 50g ball Sublime Extra Fine Merino DK shade **449 - Botanist** for contrast colour

1 x pair 3.5mm knitting needles (or the size required to give the correct tension)

1 x pair 3mm knitting needles (or a needle 0.5mm smaller than you use for main knitting)

1 x notepad and pen

1 x measuring tape

1 x scissors

1 x sewing needle

Abbreviations

cm centimetres, **C** contrast, **DK** double knitting, **g** grammes, **in** inch(es), **k** knit, **M** main, **mm** millimetres, **p** purl, **st(s)** stitch(es).

Here's how to make it ...

Check one's tension

With clean hands, cast on **22 sts** and knit **28 rows** on **3.5mm** needles or the size required to give correct tension, which should result in a **10cm (4in)** square.

If the square is bigger than this, use a thinner needle, if smaller use a thicker needle.

It's really important to get this bit correct or the hip flask cover will not result in the sizes stated.

Cast on

Using M, cast on 45 sts.

Knit the body

  1ˢᵗ Row. Knit.

  2ⁿᵈ Row. Purl.

These 2 rows form stocking stitch.

Work in stocking stitch until cover is 6cm (2 ½in) finishing after a purl row.

Change colour

Change to your smaller needles and C.

Work in stocking stitch until cover is 8cm, (3in), finishing after a purl row.

Cast off

Cast off knitways.

To serve

Join centre back seam then placing seam in centre join lower seam.

See yarn ball band for washing and further care instructions.

Use on a train journey, day in the park, anywhere a hip flask would be useful.

Share image on social media.

#knitandnibble #cover #imadethis #swig

Beer Can Cover.

Keep a can of beer cooler for longer using the natural insulating properties of wool.

Makes 1 x beer can cover in Sublime Extra Fine Merino DK.

Width x Length (approximately) 20 x 16cm (8 x 6 ¼in)

1 x 50g ball Sublime Extra Fine Merino DK shade **529 - Eucalyptus** for main colour
1 x 50g ball Sublime Extra Fine Merino DK shade **362 - Spruce** for contrast colour
1 x pair 3.5mm knitting needles (or the size required to give the correct tension)
1 x notepad and pen
1 x measuring tape
1 x scissors
1 x sewing needle

Abbreviations

cm centimetres, **C** contrast, **DK** double knitting, **g** grammes, **in** inch(es), **k** knit, **M** main, **mm** millimetres, **p** purl, **rs** right side, **st(s)** stitch(es), **ws** wrong side.

Here's how to make it …

Check one's tension

With clean hands, cast on **22 sts** and knit **42 rows** on **3.5mm** needles or the size required to give correct tension, which should result in a **10cm (4in)** square.

If the square is bigger than this, use a thinner needle, if smaller use a thicker needle.

It's really important to get this bit correct or the beer can cover will not result in the sizes stated.

Cast on

Using M, cast on 44 sts.

Knit the body

1st Row (this will be the right side of the work - **rs**). Knit.

This row forms garter stitch.

Work in garter stitch until cover is 13cm (5 ¼in) finishing after a ws row.

Change colour

Change to C and work in garter stitch until cover is 15cm (6in), finishing after a rs row.

Cast off

Cast off knitways.

To serve

Join centre back seam.

See yarn ball band for washing and further care instructions.

Add a can of beer. Summer's day. Friends. BBQ.

Post your exploits on social media.

#knitandnibble #cover #imadethis

Wine Bottle Cover.

Keep a white or rosé colder, or, hide the label on a cheeky cheap bottle of red.

Makes 1 x wine bottle cover in Sublime Extra Fine Merino DK.

Width x Length (approximately) 23 x 19cm (9 x 7½in)

1 x 50g ball Sublime Extra Fine Merino DK shade **411 - Pomeroy** for main colour
1 x 50g ball Sublime Extra Fine Merino DK shade **410 - Betty** for contrast colour
1 x pair 3.5mm knitting needles (or the size required to give the correct tension)
1 x notepad and pen
1 x measuring tape
1 x scissors
1 x sewing needle

Abbreviations

cm centimetres, **C** contrast, **DK** double knitting, **g** grammes, **in** inch(es), **k** knit, **M** main, **mm** millimetres, **p** purl, **rs** right side, **st(s)** stitch(es), **ws** wrong side.

Here's how to make it ...

Check one's tension

With clean hands, cast on **26 sts** and knit **30 rows** in 2x2 rib when stretched to correct width on **3.5mm** needles or the size required to give correct tension, which should result in a **10cm (4in)** square.

If the square is bigger than this, use a thinner needle, if smaller use a thicker needle.

It's really important to get this bit correct or the cloth will not result in the sizes stated.

Cast on

Using M, cast on 58 sts.

1st Row. * K2, p2, repeat from * to last 2 sts, k2.
2nd Row. P2, * k2, p2, repeat from * to end.

These 2 rows form 2x2 rib.

Work in rib until cover is 17cm, (6 ½in), finishing after a ws row.

Change colour

Change to C and work in rib until cover is 19cm, (7 ½in).

Cast off

Cast off in rib.

To serve

Sew up back seam.

Adorn wine bottle.

See yarn ball band for washing and further care instructions.

If made up after 6pm, serve as above, take picture and post to social media with choice of drink in hand.

#knitandnibble #cover #imadethis

Wrap.

Up warm, or a scarf as a present.

Going the extra mile is like knitting a scarf.

It may not be a mile, but knitting stamina builds up when making a scarf.

Taking what you have learnt before in this book and putting knit and purl stitches together to create a garment.

Your first project for you to wear, or give as a present.

Knit in Sirdar Harrap Tweed Chunky, Sublime Extra Fine Merino DK and Sublime Extra Fine Merino Worsted, with a choice of over 32,000 colour combinations.

- **Turn** - basket stitch scarf
- **Move** - 4x4 rib scarf
- **Go** - striped scarf with rib edges
- **Win** - football style scarf

Wrap - knitting a longer project

HARRAP TWEED

Sublime

Turn.

Makes 1 x scarf in Sirdar Harrap Tweed Chunky.

Width x Length (approximately) 18 x 150cm (7 x 59in)

3 x 100g balls Sirdar Harrap Tweed Chunky consisting of:

    2 balls for the main colour, shade **109 - Emley**

    1 ball for the contrast colour, shade **103 - Hepworth**

1 x pair of 6.5mm knitting needles (or the size required to give the correct tension)

1 x row counter

1 x notepad and pen

1 x measuring tape

1 x scissors

1 x sewing needle

Abbreviations

cm centimetres, **C** contrast, **DK** double knitting, **g** grammes, **in** inch(es), **k** knit, **M** main, **mm** millimetres, **p** purl, **st(s)** stitch(es), **ws** wrong side.

Here's how to make it ...

Check one's tension

With clean hands, cast on **14 sts** and knit **19 rows** in stocking stitch (knit one row, purl one row and repeat) on **6.5mm** needles or the size required to give correct tension, which should result in a **10cm (4in)** square.

If the square is bigger than this, use a thinner needle, if smaller use a thicker needle.

It's really important to get this bit correct or the scarf size will not result in the sizes stated.

As long as you knit the stocking stitch at the above tension, the basket weave pattern for the scarf should be the same.

Cast on

Using M, cast on 25 sts.

Learn the stitch pattern

1st Row. (this will be the right side of the work – **rs**). * K5, p5, repeat from * to last 5 sts, k5.

2nd Row. P5, * k5, p5, repeat from * to end.

Repeat 1st and 2nd rows twice more.

Change colour

** Using C, proceed as follows:

    Next Row. Knit.

    Next Row. * K5, p5, repeat from * to last 5 sts, k5.

    Next Row. P5, * k5, p5, repeat from * to end.

    Repeat last 2 rows once more.

    Next Row. * K5, p5, repeat from * to last 5 sts, k5.

Change colour

Using M, proceed as follows:

Next Row. Knit.

Next Row. * P5, k5, repeat from * to last 5 sts, p5.

Next Row. K5, * p5, k5, repeat from * to end. Repeat last 2 rows once more.

Next Row. * P5, k5, repeat from * to last 5 sts, p5. **

Repeat from ** to ** once more.

Using M, proceed as follows:

1st Row. * P5, k5, repeat from * to last 5 sts, p5.

2nd Row. K5, * p5, k5, repeat from * to end. Repeat 1st and 2nd rows twice more.

7th Row. * K5, p5, repeat from * to last 5 sts, k5.

8th Row. P5, * k5, p5, repeat from * to end. Repeat 7th and 8th rows once more then 7th row once more.

12th Row. P5, * k5, p5, repeat from * to end. From 1st to 12th row forms pattern.

Continue in pattern until scarf measures approximately 137cm, (54in), finishing after 12th row of pattern.

Repeat from ** to ** twice more.

Cast off

Cast off in pattern, using M.

To serve

Sew in ends.

Pin out scarf to measurement given and cover with damp cloths until dry.

Wrap around neck.

See yarn ball band for washing and further care instructions.

Add any of the jumpers featured in this book, a warm overcoat and don't forget to knit a hat.

Post to social media. Have you joined ravelry.com - the knitters social network?

#knitandnibble #scarf #imadethis

Move.

Makes 1 x scarf in Sublime Extra Fine Merino DK.

Width x Length (approximately) 26 x 160cm (10 ¼ x 63 ¼in)

6 x 50g balls Sublime Extra Fine Merino DK consisting of:

    4 balls of colour A, shade **010 - Salt Grey**

    1 ball of colour B, shade **446 - Duffy**

    1 ball of colour C, shade **409 - Blackcurrant**

1 x pair of 4mm knitting needles (or the size required to give the correct tension)

1 x pair of 4.5mm knitting needles (or the size required to give the correct tension)

1 x row counter

1 x notepad and pen

1 x measuring tape

1 x scissors

1 x sewing needle

Abbreviations

cm centimetres, **C** contrast, **DK** double knitting, **g** grammes, **in** inch(es), **k** knit, **M** main, **mm** millimetres, **p** purl, **st(s)** stitch(es), **ws** wrong side.

Here's how to make it ...

Check one's tension

With clean hands, cast on **22 sts** and knit **28 rows** in stocking stitch (knit one row, purl one row and repeat) on **4mm** needles or the size required to give correct tension, which should result in a **10cm (4in)** square.

If the square is bigger than this, use a thinner needle, if smaller use a thicker needle.

As long as you knit the stocking stitch at the above tension the ribbed pattern should be **23 sts** and **26 rows** to 10cm (4in) using **4.5mm** needles when slightly stretched.

It's really important to get this bit correct or the scarf size will not result in the sizes stated.

Cast on

Using your larger needles and A, cast on 60 sts.

Knit the rib pattern

1st Row. (this will be the right side of the work –

rs) * K4, p4, repeat from * to last 4 sts, k4.

2nd Row. P4, * k4, p4, repeat from * to end.

These 2 rows form 4x4 rib pattern.

Repeat these 2 rows until scarf measures approximately 6cm, (2½in), finishing after 2nd row of rib pattern.

Work rib pattern and stripe sequence as follows:

Stripe Sequence

** Work 2 rows in B,

2 rows in C,

2 rows in B,

10 rows in A,

2 rows in B,

2 rows in C,

2 rows in B

and 12cm, (4 ¾in) in A.

**Beginning with stripe sequence repeat from ** to ** 6 times more.

Work 2 rows in B,

2 rows in C,

2 rows in B,

10 rows in A,

2 rows in B,

2 rows in C,

2 rows in B

and 6cm, (2 ½in) in A only, finishing after 2nd row of rib pattern.

Cast off

Cast off in rib.

To serve

Sew in ends.

Pin out scarf to measurement given and cover with damp cloths until dry.

Wrap around neck.

See yarn ball band for washing and further care instructions.

Add any of the jumpers featured in this book, a warm overcoat and don't forget to knit a hat.

#knitandnibble #scarf #imadethis

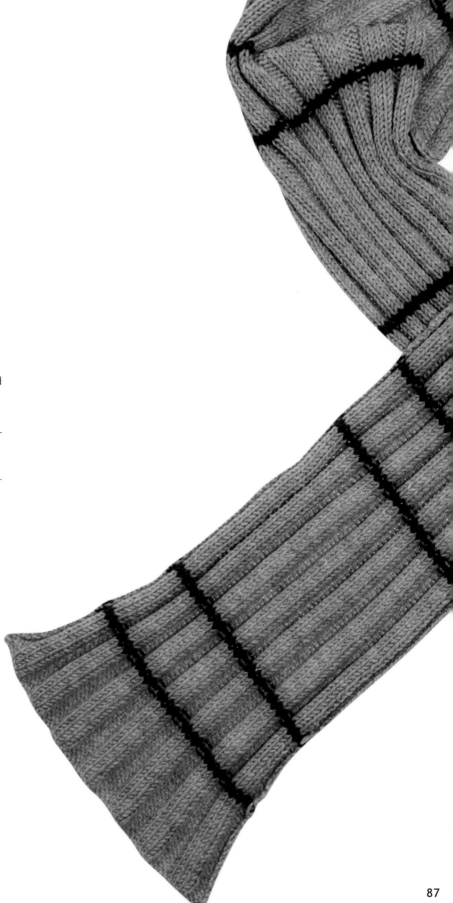

Go.

Makes 1 x scarf in Sublime Extra Fine Merino Worsted.

Width x Length (approximately) 21 x 177cm (8¼ x 69¾in)

7 x 50g balls Sublime Extra Fine Merino Worsted consisting of:
    4 balls of colour A, shade **062 - Aubergine**
    1 ball of colour B, shade **554 - Marni**
    1 ball of colour C, shade **228 - Roasted Pepper**
    1 ball of colour D, shade **579 - Margot**
1 x pair of 4.5mm knitting needles (or the size required to give the correct tension)
1 x row counter
1 x notepad and pen
1 x measuring tape
1 x scissors
1 x sewing needle

Abbreviations

cm centimetres, **C** contrast, **DK** double knitting, **g** grammes, **in** inch(es), **k** knit, **M** main, **mm** millimetres, **p** purl, **st(s)** stitch(es), **ws** wrong side.

Here's how to make it ...

Check one's tension

With clean hands, cast on **18 sts** and knit **24 rows** in stocking stitch (knit one row, purl one row and repeat) on **4.5mm** needles or the size required to give correct tension, which should result in a **10cm (4in)** square.

If the square is bigger than this, use a thinner needle, if smaller use a thicker needle.

It's really important to get this bit correct or the scarf size will not result in the sizes stated.

Cast on

Using A, cast on 38 sts.

Knit the rib pattern

1st Row. (This will be the right side of the work – **rs**). (K1, p1) 3 times, * k2, p2, repeat from * to last 8 sts, k2, (p1, k1) 3 times.

2nd Row. (P1, k1) 3 times, p2, * k2, p2, repeat from * to last 6 sts, (k1, p1) 3 times.

These 2 rows form rib.

Repeat 1st and 2nd rows 3 times more.

Knit the main pattern

1st Row. (K1, p1) 3 times, knit to last 6 sts, (p1, k1) 3 times.

2nd Row. (P1, k1) 3 times, purl to last 6 sts, (k1, p1) 3 times.

These 2 rows form pattern.

Repeat them 3 times more.

Keeping continuity of main pattern proceed as follows:

Stripe Sequence

Work 2 rows in B,

4 rows in C,

4 rows in D,

4 rows in C,

4 rows in D,

4 rows in C,

4 rows in D,

4 rows in C

and 2 rows in B.

Using A, work a further 61cm, (24in), finishing after a ws row.

(Work 4 rows in B, 4 rows in A) 4 times then 4 rows in B.

Using A only, work a further 61cm, (24in), finishing after a ws row.

Work 2 rows in B,

4 rows in C,

4 rows in D,

4 rows in C,

4 rows in D,

4 rows in C,

4 rows in D,

4 rows in C

and 2 rows in B.

Using A, work 8 rows in main pattern.

Starting with 1st row of rib pattern work 8 rows.

Cast off

Cast off in rib.

To serve

Sew in ends.

Pin out scarf to measurement given and cover with damp cloths until dry.

Wrap around neck.

See yarn ball band for washing and further care instructions.

Add any of the jumpers featured in this book, a warm overcoat and don't forget to knit a hat.

Now decide where you want to go.

#knitandnibble #scarf #imadethis

Win.

Makes 1 x scarf in Sublime Extra Fine Merino Worsted.

Width x Length (approximately) 20 x 169cm (8 x 66¾in)

8 x 50g balls Sublime Extra Fine Merino Worsted consisting of:

    4 balls of colour A, shade **539 - Charleston**

    4 balls of colour B, shade **003 - Alabaster**

1 x pair of 4.5mm knitting needles (or the size required to give the correct tension)

1 x row counter

1 x notepad and pen

1 x measuring tape

1 x scissors

1 x sewing needle

Abbreviations

cm centimetres, **C** contrast, **DK** double knitting, **g** grammes, **in** inch(es), **k** knit, **M** main, **mm** millimetres, **p** purl, **st(s)** stitch(es), **ws** wrong side.

Here's how to make it ...

Check one's tension

With clean hands, cast on **18 sts** and knit **24 rows** in stocking stitch (knit one row, purl one row and repeat) on **4.5mm** needles or the size required to give correct tension, which should result in a **10cm (4in)** square.

If the square is bigger than this, use a thinner needle, if smaller use a thicker needle.

It's really important to get this bit correct or the scarf size will not result in the sizes stated.

Cast on

Using A, cast on 72 sts.

Knit the stripes

Working in stocking stitch (throughout) proceed as follows:

    work 14 rows in A.

Proceed as follows:

Stripe Sequence
** Work 14 rows in B and 14 rows in A. **
Repeat from ** to ** 13 times more.

Cast off

Cast off knit wise.

To serve

Fold scarf in half lengthways and sew seam at centre back of scarf.

Sew ends together.

Using B and 4 strands of yarn 20cm (8in) in length, fringe evenly along each end of scarf as shown in diagram in left corner if required.

Pin out scarf to the measurements given and cover with damp cloths until dry.

Wrap around neck, go to the match, raise scarf above your head, yell 'here we go,' enjoy.

See yarn ball band for washing and further care instructions.

Add sports kit. Match tickets. Beer can holder.

If made up after 6pm, serve as above, take picture at match and post to social media.

#knitandnibble #scarf
#herewegoherewego #imadethis

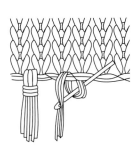

Sublime

Grab.

Your hat. Put it on

But first you need to knit it, shape it, and sew it up

Knit in Sublime Extra Fine Merino DK

Choose over 465 colour combinations

- Slouchy
- Beanie

Grab - learning about decreasing

Slouchy.

Makes 1 x slouchy hat in Sublime Extra Fine Merino DK to fit an average size adult head.

2 x 50g balls Sublime Extra Fine Merino DK consisting of:

    1 ball of shade **409 - Blackcurrant** for main colour

    1 ball of shade **364 - Black Cherry** for contrast colour

1 x pair of 4mm knitting needles (or the size required to give the correct tension for main knitting)

1 x pair of 3.5mm knitting needles (or a needle 0.5mm smaller than you use for main knitting)

1 x row counter

1 x notepad and pen

1 x measuring tape

1 x scissors

1 x sewing needle

Abbreviations

cm centimetres, **C** contrast, **DK** double knitting, **g** grammes, **in** inch(es), **k** knit, **M** main, **mm** millimetres, **p** purl, **st(s)** stitch(es), **tog** together, **K2tog** insert the right-hand needle through the 2nd and 1st stitches on the left-hand needle and knit them together to form a single stitch, **P2tog** insert the right-hand needle purlways through the 1st and 2nd stitches on the left-hand needle and purl them together to form a single stitch.

Here's how to make it ...

Check one's tension

With clean hands, cast on **22 sts** and knit **28 rows** in stocking stitch (knit one row, purl one row and repeat) on **4mm** needles or the size required to give correct tension, which should result in a **10cm (4in)** square.

If the square is bigger than this, use a thinner needle, if smaller use a thicker needle.

It's really important to get this bit correct or the hat size will not result in the correct size stated.

Cast on

Using your smaller needles and C, cast on 126 sts.

Knit the rib

1st Row. (This will be the wrong side of the work – **ws**). P2, * k2, p2, repeat from * to end.

2nd Row. * K2, p2, repeat from * to last 2 sts, k2.

These 2 rows form **2x2 rib.**

Work in 2x2 rib for 11cm, (4¼in), finishing after a rs row.

Decrease a row

Next Row. P5, p2tog, (p4, p2tog) 19 times, p5.

106 sts on the needle

Knit to main body

Change to your main needles and M.
Beginning with a knit row work in stocking
stitch for the remainder of the hat as follows:

work until hat measures 24cm, (9½in),
finishing after a ws row.

Shape the crown

Shape the crown as follows:

Next Row. K1, (k2tog, k5) 15 times.

91 sts on the needle

Work 5 rows without shaping.
Next Row. K1, (k2tog, k4) 15 times.

76 sts on the needle

Work 3 rows without shaping.
Next Row. K1, (k2tog, k3) 15 times.

61 sts on the needle

Work 3 rows without shaping.
Next Row. K1, (k2tog, k2) 15 times.

46 sts on the needle

Work 3 rows without shaping.
Next Row. K1, (k2tog, k1) 15 times.

31 sts on the needle

Work 3 rows without shaping.
Next Row. K1, (k2tog) 15 times.

16 sts on the needle

Next Row. (P2tog) 8 times.

8 sts on the needle

Cast off

Break off yarn, run yarn through remaining 8
sts, draw up and fasten off.

To serve

Join back seam, reversing sewing for turnback.

Cover with a damp cloth until dry. Put on head,
go outside. Don't forget an umbrella if it's
raining.

See yarn ball band for washing and further
care instructions.

If made up after 6pm, serve as above, take
picture of you in your new hat - post to social
media.

#knitandnibble #slouchyhat #imadethis

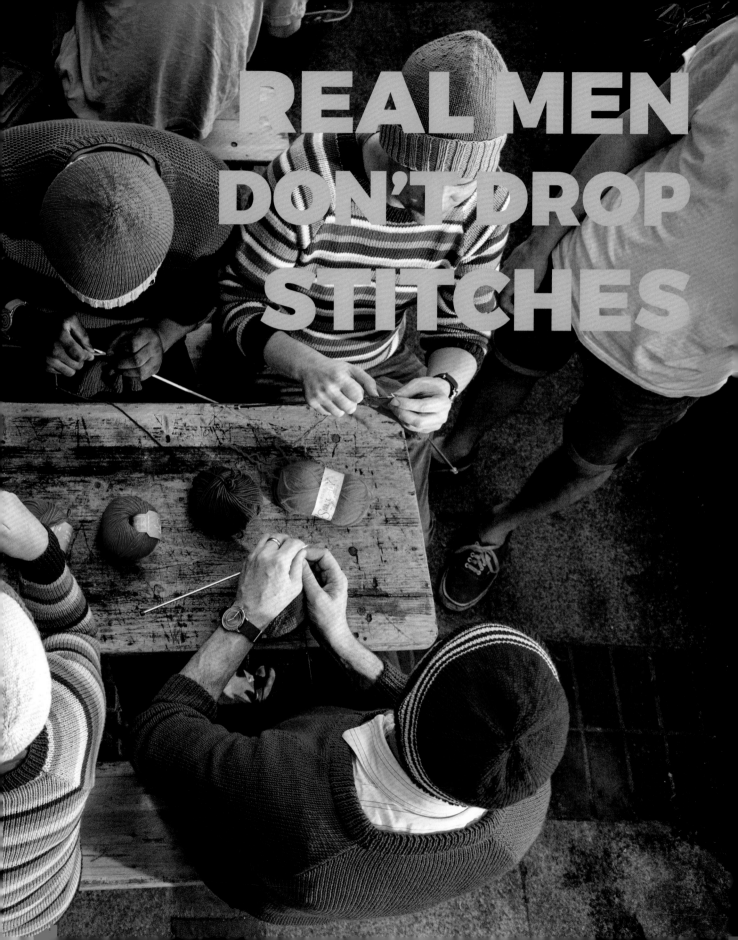

Beanie.

Makes 1 x beanie hat in Sublime Extra Fine Merino DK to fit an average size adult head.

2 x 50g balls Sublime Extra Fine Merino DK consisting of:

  1 ball of shade **363 - Indigo** for main colour

  1 ball of shade **003 - Alabaster** for contrast colour

1 x pair of 4mm knitting needles (or the size required to give the correct tension for main knitting)

1 x pair of 3.5mm knitting needles (or a needle 0.5mm smaller than you use for main knitting)

1 x row counter

1 x notepad and pen

1 x measuring tape

1 x scissors

1 x sewing needle

Abbreviations

cm centimetres, **C** contrast, **DK** double knitting, **g** grammes, **in** inch(es), **k** knit, **M** main, **mm** millimetres, **p** purl, **st(s)** stitch(es), **tog** together, **K2tog** insert the right-hand needle through the 2nd and 1st stitches on the left-hand needle and knit them together to form a single stitch, **P2tog** insert the right-hand needle purlways through the 1st and 2nd stitches on the left-hand needle and purl them together to form a single stitch.

Here's how to make it ...

Check one's tension

With clean hands, cast on **22 sts** and knit **28 rows** in stocking stitch (knit one row, purl one row and repeat) on **4mm** needles or the size required to give correct tension, which should result in a **10cm (4in)** square.

If the square is bigger than this, use a thinner needle, if smaller use a thicker needle.

It's really important to get this bit correct or the hat size will not result in the correct size stated.

Cast on

Using your smaller needles and M, cast on 145 sts.

Knit the rib

1st Row. (This will be the right side of the work – **rs**). * K1, p1, repeat from * to last st, k1.

2nd Row. P1, * k1, p1, repeat from * to end.

These 2 rows form **1x1 rib**.

Work 9 rows more in 1x1 rib.

Decrease a row

Next Row. P8, p2tog, (p4, p2tog) 21 times, p9.

123 sts on the needle

Knit to main body

Change to your main needles and C.

Proceed as follows:

1st Row. (This will be the right side of the work – rs). Knit.
Change to M.
2nd Row. Purl.
Change to C.
3rd Row. Knit.
4th Row. Purl.
Change to M.
5th Row. Knit.
6th Row. Purl.
Change to C.
7th Row. Knit.
8th Row. Purl.
9th Row. Knit.
Change to M.
10th Row. Purl.
11th Row. Knit.
12th Row. Purl.
Change to C.
13th Row. Knit.
14th Row. Purl.
Change to M.
15th Row. Knit.
16th Row. Purl.
Change to C.
17th Row. Knit.
Change to M.

Beginning with a purl row work in stocking stitch for the remainder of the hat as follows:

work until hat measures 14cm, (5½in), finishing after a rs row.

Next Row. Purl to end decreasing 2 sts evenly across row.

121 sts on the needle

Shape the crown

Shape the crown as follows:

Next Row. K1, (k2tog, k4) 20 times.

101 sts on the needle

Work 7 rows without shaping.
Next Row. K1, (k2tog, k3) 20 times.

81 sts on the needle

Work 5 rows without shaping.

Next Row. K1, (k2tog, k2) 20 times.

61 sts on the needle

Work 3 rows without shaping.
Next Row. K1, (k2tog, k1) 20 times.

41 sts on the needle

Work 3 rows without shaping.
Next Row. K1, (k2tog) 20 times.

21 sts on the needle

Next Row. (P2tog) 10 times, p1.

11 sts on the needle

Cast off

Break off yarn, run yarn through remaining 11 sts, draw up and fasten off.

To serve

Join back seam.

Cover with a damp cloth until dry.

Put on head, add a scarf in matching or contrast colours - go outside.

See yarn ball band for washing and further care instructions.

If made up after 6pm, serve as above, take selfie and post to social media with choice of drink in hand.

#knitandnibble #beaniehat #imadethis

Smart.

Look smart. Sleeves not required

A jumper without sleeves

Knit in Sirdar Harrap Tweed DK, with a choice of 12 colours

- Round neck tank top
- V-neck tank top

Tank - shaping a project, neckline, armholes and edging

HARRAP TWEED

Smart.

Makes 1 x tank top in Sirdar Harrap Tweed DK as either a round or V-neck.

Sirdar Harrap Tweed DK 50g balls of yarn:

    Round neck 5 [6:6:7:7:7] shade **103 - Hepworth**

    V-neck 5 [5:6:6:6:7] shade **101 - Simpson**

1 x pair of 4mm knitting needles (or the size required to give the correct tension)

1 x pair of 3.5mm knitting needles (or a needle 0.5mm smaller than you use for main knitting)

1 x row counter

1 x notepad and pen

1 x measuring tape

2 x stitch holders

1 x stitch marker or safety pin for V-neck

1 x scissors

1 x sewing needle

Abbreviations

cm centimetres, **DK** double knitting, **g** grammes, **in** inch(es), **k** knit, **mm** millimetres, **0** no rows, **p** purl, **st(s)** stitch(es), **tog** together, **K2tog** insert the right-hand needle knitways through 2nd and 1st stitches on the left-hand needle and knit them together to form a single stitch, **P2tog** insert the right-hand needle purlways through the 1st and 2nd stitches on the left-hand needle and purl them together to form a single stitch.

Size

To Fit Chest	cm	97	102	107	**112**	117	122
	in	38	40	42	**44**	46	48
Actual Size	cm	94	99	103	**108**	114	119
	in	37	39	40 ½	**42 ½**	45	47
Full Length	cm	66	68	70	**71**	72	73
	in	26	26 ¾	27 ½	**28**	28 ¼	28 ¾

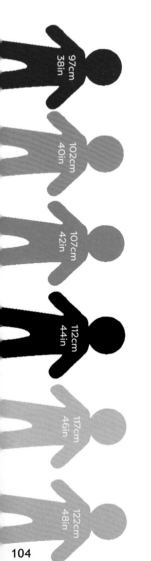

97cm 38in

102cm 40in

107cm 42in

112cm 44in

117cm 46in

122cm 48in

Round neck

Here's how to make it …

Check one's tension

With clean hands, cast on **22 sts** and knit **28 rows** in stocking stitch (knit one row, purl one row and repeat) on **4mm** needles or the size required to give correct tension, which should result in a **10cm (4in)** square.

If the square is bigger than this, use a thinner needle, if smaller use a thicker needle.

It's really important to get this bit correct or the tank top size will not result in the sizes stated.

Knit the back

Using your smaller needles cast on **121** [**127**:**133**:**141**:147:153] sts.

1st Row. (This will be the right side of the work – **rs**). * K1, p1, repeat from * to last st, k1.

2nd Row. P1, * k1, p1, repeat from * to end.

1st and 2nd rows form **1x1 rib**.

Work 13 rows more in 1x1 rib.

Next Row. P8 [3:8:6:9:2], p2tog, (p4 [5:4:4:4:5], p2tog) **17** [17:19:21:21:21] times, p9 [3:9:7:10:2]. ***

103 [109:113:119:125:131] sts on the needle

Change to your main needles and beginning with a knit row work in stocking stitch for the remainder of the back as follows:

work until back measures **43** [**44**:**45**:**45**:45:45]cm, (**17** [17¼:17¾:**17¾**:17¼:17¾]in), finishing after a wrong side row.

Shape armholes

Cast off **6** [**6**:**6**:**7**:7:8] sts at beginning of the next 2 rows.

91 [97:101:105:111:115] sts on the needle

Work **4** [**4**:**4**:**6**:6:6] rows decreasing 1 st at each end of every row.

83 [89:93:93:99:103] sts on the needle

Work **5** [**7**:**7**:**5**:5:7] rows decreasing 1 st at each end of 1st and every following alternate row. **

77 [81:85:87:93:95] sts on the needle

Continue without further shaping until armholes measures **23** [**24**:**25**:**26**:27:28]cm, (**9** [9½:9¾:**10¼**:10¾:11]in), straight down from the top of the needle to the beginning of the armhole shaping (don't measure around the curve),

finishing after a wrong side row.

Shape shoulders

Cast off **10** [**11**:**11**:**11**:12:12] sts at beginning of the next 2 rows.

57 [59:63:65:69:71] sts on the needle

Cast off **10** [**11**:**11**:**12**:12:13] sts at beginning the next 2 rows.

37 [37:41:41:45:45] sts on the needle

Slip remaining **37** [**37**:**41**:**41**:45:45] sts onto a stitch holder.

Knit the front

Work as given for back to. **

Continue without further shaping until armholes measure **13** [**13**:**14**:**15**:16:17]cm, (**5¼** [5¼:5½:**6**:6¼:6½]in), finishing after a wrong side row.

Divide for neck

Next Row. K**30** [**31**:**33**:**34**:35:36], turn, slip remaining **47** [**50**:**52**:**53**:58:59] sts onto a stitch holder. You will come back to these **47** [**50**:**52**:**53**:58:59] sts later to work the second side of the neck.

30 [31:33:34:35:36] sts on the needle

Next Row. Purl.

Work 4 rows decreasing 1 st at neck edge in every row.

26 [27:29:30:31:32] sts on the needle

Work **11** [**9**:**13**:**13**:13:13] rows decreasing 1 st at neck edge in 1st and every following alternate row.

20 [22:22:23:24:25] sts on the needle

Continue without further shaping until armhole measures same as back armhole to shoulder shaping, finishing after a wrong side row.

Shape shoulder

Next Row. Cast off **10** [**11**:**11**:**11**:12:12] sts, knit to end.

10 [11:11:12:12:13] sts on the needle

Next Row. Purl.

Cast off remaining **10** [**11**:**11**:**12**:12:13] sts.

To work the second side of the neck, return the **47** [**50**:**52**:**53**:58:59] sts left on a stitch holder onto the needle. With the rs of the work facing you, slip **17** [**19**:**19**:**19**:23:23] sts onto a stitch holder, rejoin yarn to remaining **30** [**31**:**33**:**34**:35:36] sts and knit to end.

30 [31:33:34:35:36] sts on the needle

Next Row. Purl.

Work 4 rows decreasing 1 st at neck edge in every row.

26 [27:29:30:31:32] sts on the needle

Work **11** [**9**:**13**:**13**:13:13] rows decreasing 1 st at neck edge in 1st and every following alternate row.

20 [**22**:**22**:**23**:24:25] sts on the needle

Continue without further shaping until armhole measures same as Back armhole to shoulder shaping, finishing after a rs row.

Next Row. Cast off **10** [**11**:**11**:**11**:12:12] sts, purl to end.

10 [**11**:**11**:**12**:12:13] sts on the needle

Next Row. Knit.

Cast off remaining **10** [**11**:**11**:**12**:12:13] sts.

Knit the neckband

Join right shoulder seam. With the rs of the work facing you, using your smaller needles, pick up and knit **28** [**31**:**31**:**31**:31:31] sts evenly down left side of neck, work across **17** [**19**:**19**:**19**:23:23] sts left on a stitch holder at front of neck as follows:

> k**5** [**6**:**6**:**6**:7:7], pick up loop between last and next stitch and knit into the back of this loop (this will now be referred to as **m1**), k**7** [**7**:**7**:**7**:9:9], m1, k**5** [**6**:**6**:**6**:7:7], pick up and knit **28** [**31**:**31**:**31**:31:31] sts evenly up right side of neck and work across **37** [**37**:**41**:**41**:45:45] sts left on a stitch holder at back of neck as follows:
> > k**3** [**3**:**5**:**5**:7:7], m1, (k5, m1) 6 times, k**4** [**4**:**6**:**6**:8:8].

119 [**127**:**131**:**131**:139:139] sts on the needle

Beginning with 2nd row of 1x1 rib, work 7 rows.

Cast off in rib.

Knit the armhole borders, both alike

Join left shoulder and neckband seams. With the rs of the work facing you, using your smaller needles, pick up and knit **125** [**129**:**135**:**143**:147:153] sts evenly all round armhole edge.

Beginning with 2nd row of 1x1 rib, work 7 rows.

Cast off in rib.

To serve

Join side and armhole border seams. Pin out garment to measurements given and cover with damp cloths until dry. See yarn ball band for washing and further care instructions.

Wear with a nice shirt underneath.

#knitandnibble #tanktop #imadethis

V-neck

Here's how to make it ...

Knit the back

Work as given for back of round neck tank top to. ***

Change to your main needles and beginning with a knit row work in stocking stitch for the remainder of the back as follows:

work until back measures **41** [**42**:**43**:**43**:43:43]cm, (**16** [**16½**:**17**:**17**:17:17]in), finishing after a wrong side row. ****

Work 6 rows more.

Shape armholes

Cast off **6** [**6**:**6**:**7**:**7**:8] sts at beginning of the next 2 rows.

91 [**97**:**101**:**105**:111:115] sts on the needle

Work **4** [**4**:**4**:**6**:6:6] rows decreasing 1 st at each end of every row.

83 [**89**:**93**:**93**:99:103] sts on the needle

Work **5** [**7**:**7**:**5**:5:7] rows decreasing 1 st at each end of 1st and every following alternate row.

77 [**81**:**85**:**87**:93:95] sts on the needle

Continue without further shaping until armholes measures **23** [**24**:**25**:**26**:27:28]cm, (**9** [**9½**:**9¾**:**10¼**:10¾:11]in), straight down from the top of the needle to the beginning of the armhole shaping (don't measure around the curve), finishing after a wrong side row.

Shape shoulders

Cast off **10** [**11**:**11**:**11**:12:12] sts at beginning of the next 2 rows.

57 [**59**:**63**:**65**:69:71] sts on the needle

Cast off **10** [**11**:**11**:**12**:12:13] sts at beginning the next 2 rows.

37 [**37**:**41**:**41**:45:45] sts on the needle

Slip remaining **37** [**37**:**41**:**41**:45:45] sts onto a stitch holder.

Knit the front

Work as given for back to. ****

Divide for neck

Next Row. K**49** [**52**:**54**:**57**:60:63], k2tog, turn, slip remaining **52** [**55**:**57**:**60**:63:66] sts onto a stitch holder. You will come back to these **52** [**55**:**57**:**60**:63:66] sts later to work the second side of the neck.

50 [**53**:**55**:**58**:61:64] sts on the needle

Next Row. Purl.

Next Row. Knit to last 2 sts, k2tog.

49 [**52**:**54**:**57**:60:63] sts on the needle

Next Row. Purl.

Work 2 rows decreasing 1 st at neck edge in 1st row.

48 [**51**:**53**:**56**:59:62] sts on the needle

Shape armhole

Next Row. Cast off **6** [**6**:**6**:**7**:7:8] sts, knit to last 2 sts, k2tog.

41 [**44**:**46**:**48**:51:53] sts on the needle

Next Row. Purl.

For 1st, 2nd, 3rd and 4th sizes only

Work **4** [**4**:**4**:**6**] rows decreasing 1 st at armhole edge in every row **AT SAME TIME** decrease 1 st at neck edge in **1st** [**3rd**:**1st**:**1st**] and following **0** [**0**:**2nd**:**2nd**] row.

36 [**39**:**40**:**40**] sts on the needle

For 5th and 6th sizes only

Work 6 rows decreasing 1 st at armhole edge in every row **AT SAME TIME** decrease 1 st at neck edge in 1st and every following 2nd row.

[42:44] sts on the needle

For all 6 sizes

Work **6** [**8**:**8**:**6**:6:8] rows decreasing 1 st at armhole edge in 1st and every following alternate row **AT SAME TIME** decrease 1 st at neck edge in **1st** [**3rd**:**1st**:**1st**:1st:3rd] and following **4th** [**4th**:**4th**:**4th**:2nd:4th] row.

31 [**33**:**34**:**35**:37:38] sts on the needle

Work **43** [**43**:**45**:**47**:49:51] rows decreasing 1 st at neck edge only in **3rd** [**3rd**:**1st**:**3rd**:1st:3rd] and every following 4th row.

20 [**22**:**22**:**23**:24:25] sts on the needle

Continue without further shaping until armhole measures same as back armhole to shoulder shaping, finishing after a wrong side row.

Shape shoulders

Next Row. Cast off **10** [**11**:**11**:**11**:12:12] sts, knit to end.

10 [**11**:**11**:**12**:12:13] sts on the needle

Next Row. Purl.

Cast off remaining **10** [**11**:**11**:**12**:12:13] sts.

To work the second side of the neck, return the **52** [**55**:**57**:**60**:63:66] sts left on a stitch holder to the needle. With rs of the work facing you, slip 1 st onto a stitch marker or safety pin, rejoin yarn to remaining **51** [**54**:**56**:**59**:62:65] sts k2tog, knit to end.

50 [**53**:**55**:**58**:61:64] sts on the needle

Next Row. Purl.

Next Row. K2tog, knit to end.

49 [**52**:**54**:**57**:60:63] sts on the needle

Next Row. Purl.

Work 3 rows decreasing 1 st at neck edge in 1st and following alternate row.

47 [**50**:**52**:**55**:58:61] sts on the needle

Shape armhole

Next Row. Cast off **6** [**6**:**6**:**7**:7:8] sts, purl to end.

41 [**44**:**46**:**48**:51:53] sts on the needle

For 1st, 2nd, 3rd and 4th sizes only

Work **4** [**4**:**4**:**6**] rows decreasing 1 st at neck edge in **1st** [**3rd**:**1st**:**1st**] and following **0** [**0**:**2nd**:**2nd**] row **AT SAME TIME** decrease 1 st at armhole edge in every row.

36 [**39**:**40**:**40**] sts on the needle

For 5th and 6th sizes only

Work 6 rows decreasing 1 st at neck edge in 1st and every following 2nd row **AT SAME TIME** decrease 1 st at armhole edge in every row.

[42:44] sts on the needle

For all 6 sizes

Work **6** [**8**:**8**:**6**:6:8] rows decreasing 1 st at neck edge in **1st** [**3rd**:**1st**:**1st**:1st:**3rd**] and following **4th**[**4th**:**4th**:**4th**:**4th**:2nd:**4th**]row **AT SAME TIME** decrease 1 st at armhole edge in 1st and every following alternate row.

31 [**33**:**34**:**35**:37:38] sts on the needle

Work **43** [**43**:**45**:**47**:49:51] rows decreasing 1 st at neck edge only in **3rd** [**3rd**:**1st**:**3rd**:1st:**3rd**] and every following 4th row.

20 [**22**:**22**:**23**:24:25] sts on the needle

Continue without further shaping until armhole measures same as back armhole to shoulder shaping, finishing after a rs row.

Next Row. Cast off **10** [**11**:**11**:**11**:12:12] sts, purl to end.

10 [**11**:**11**:**12**:12:13] sts on the needle

Next Row. Knit.

Cast off remaining **10** [**11**:**11**:**12**:12:13] sts.

Knit the neckband

Join right shoulder seam. With the rs of the work facing you, using your smaller needles, pick up and knit 66 [70:72:74:78:80] sts evenly down left side of neck, knit stitch left on a safety pin at centre of V, pick up and knit 66 [70:72:72:74:78:80] sts evenly up right side of neck and work across 37 [37:41:41:45:45] sts left on a stitch holder at back of neck as follows:

k17 [17:19:19:21:21], k2tog, k18 [18:20:20:22:22].

169 [177:185:189:201:205] sts on the needle

1st Row. (P1, k1) 50 [52:55:56:60:61] times, p1, insert needle purlways through back of 2nd st then 1st st on left-hand needle and slip both sts off needle together, p1, pass 2 slipped sts together over purl st, p1, (k1, p1) 32 [34:35:36:38:39] times.

167 [175:183:187:199:203] sts on the needle

2nd Row. (K1, p1) 32 [34:35:36:38:39] times, insert needle knitways into 2nd st then 1st st and slip both sts off needle together, k1, pass 2 slipped sts together over knit st, (p1, k1) 50 [52:55:56:60:61] times.

165 [173:181:185:197:201] sts on the needle

3rd Row. (P1, k1) 49 [51:54:55:59:60] times, p1, insert needle purlways through back of 2nd st then 1st st on left-hand needle and slip both sts off needle together, k1, pass 2 slipped sts together over knit st, p1, (k1, p1) 31 [33:34:35:37:38] times.

163 [171:179:183:195:199] sts on the needle

4th Row. (K1, p1) 31 [33:34:35:37:38] times, insert needle knitways into 2nd st then 1st st and slip both sts off needle together, k1, pass 2 slipped sts together over purl st, (p1, k1) 49 [51:54:55:59:60] times.

161 [169:177:181:193:197] sts on the needle

5th Row. (P1, k1) 48 [50:53:54:58:59] times, p1, insert needle purlways through back of 2nd st then 1st st on left-hand needle and slip both sts off needle together, k1, pass 2 slipped sts together over knit st, p1, (k1, p1) 30 [32:33:34:36:37] times.

159 [167:175:179:191:195] sts on the needle

6th Row. (K1, p1) 30 [32:33:34:36:37] times, insert needle knitways into 2nd st then 1st st and slip both sts off needle

together, k1, pass 2 slipped sts together over knit st, (p1, k1) 48 [50:53:54:58:59] times.

157 [165:173:177:189:193] sts on the needle

7th Row. (P1, k1) 47 [49:52:53:57:58] times, p1, insert needle purlways through back of 2nd st then 1st st on left-hand needle and slip both sts off needle together, k1, pass 2 slipped sts together over knit st, p1, (k1, p1) 29 [31:32:33:35:36] times.

155 [163:171:175:187:191] sts on the needle

Cast off in rib decreasing 2 sts at centre of V as before.

Knit the armhole borders, both alike

Work as given for armhole borders of round neck tank top.

To serve

Join left shoulder and neckband seams.

Pin out garment to the measurements given and cover with damp cloths until dry. Wear over a nice shirt.

See yarn ball band for washing and further care instructions.

If made up after 6pm, serve as above, take picture and post to social media with choice of drink in hand.

#knitandnibble #tanktop #imadethis

Jumper
Sweater
Pullover

You decide what you call it.

Over a shirt or t-shirt, or next to the skin.

- Wear
- Tone
- Show
- Stripe
- Pour
- Calculate

Jumper. Sweater. Pullover. Learning about sleeves

Wear.

It's what you do with a jumper

A classic jumper with a choice of round or V-neck, with raglan sleeves and accenting colours.

Knit in Sublime Extra Fine Merino DK, with a choice of 435 colour combinations.

- 1 x round neck
- 1 x V-neck

Sublime
extra fine merino wool dk

Wear.

Makes 1 x classic raglan jumper in Sublime Extra Fine Merino DK.

Round neck
11 [**12**:**13**:**14**:14:15] x 50g balls Sublime Extra Fine Merino DK
main colour shade, **409 - Blackcurrant**
1 [1:1:1:1:1] x 50g ball Sublime Extra Fine Merino DK
contrast colour shade, **410 - Betty**

V-neck
11 [**12**:**13**:**14**:14:15] x 50g balls Sublime Extra Fine Merino DK
main colour shade, **015 - Clipper**
1 [1:1:1:1:1] x 50g ball Sublime Extra Fine Merino DK,
contrast colour shade, **411 - Pomeroy**

Both
1 x pair of 4mm knitting needles (or the size required to give the correct tension for main knitting)
1 x pair of 3.5mm knitting needles (or a needle 0.5mm smaller than you use for main knitting)
1 x row counter
1 x notepad and pen
1 x measuring tape
4 x stitch holders
1 x scissors
1 x sewing needle
1 x stitch marker or safety pin (V-neck only)

Abbreviations
cm centimetres, **C** contrast, **DK** double knitting, **g** grammes, **in** inch(es), **k** knit, **M** main, **mm** millimetres, **O** no rows, **p** purl, **st(s)** stitch(es), **tbl** through back of loop, **tog** together, **K2tog** insert the right-hand needle through the 2nd and 1st stitches on the left-hand needle and knit them together to form a single stitch, **P2tog** insert the right-hand needle through the 1st and 2nd stitches on the left-hand needle and purl them together to form a single stitch, **P2togtbl** insert the right-hand needle purlways through the back loops of 2nd and 1st stitches on the left-hand needle from left to right and purl them together to form a single stitch, **S1** slip 1 stitch knitways – insert the right-hand needle into next stitch as if to knit but just slip it off the left-hand needle onto the right-hand needle without working, **Psso** pass slipped stitch over – pass the slipped stitch from the right-hand needle over the stitch or stitches you have just worked, **M1** make 1 stitch knitways – pick up loop between last and next stitch and knit into the back of this loop.

Size

To Fit Chest	cm	97	102	107	**112**	117	122
	in	**38**	40	42	**44**	46	48
Actual Size	cm	97	103	108	**112**	117	123
	in	**38**	40 ½	40 ½	**44**	46	48 ½
Full Length	cm	68	70	72	**73**	74	75
	in	**26 ¾**	27 ½	28 ¼	**28 ¾**	29 ¼	29 ½
Sleeve Length	cm	47	48	48	**49**	50	51
	in	**18 ½**	19	19	**19 ¼**	19 ¾	20

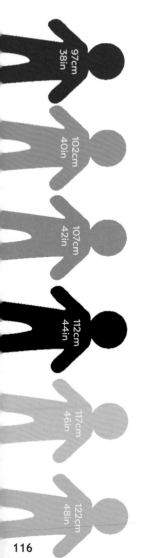

Round neck

Here's how to make it ...

Check one's tension

With clean hands, cast on **22 sts** and knit **28 rows** in stocking stitch (knit one row, purl one row and repeat) on **4mm** needles or the size required to give correct tension, which should result in a **10cm (4in)** square.

If the square is bigger than this, use a thinner needle, if smaller use a thicker needle.

It's really important to get this bit correct or the jumper size will not result in the correct size stated.

Knit the back

Using your smaller needles and C, cast on **127 [133:139:145: 153:159]** sts.

Change to M and proceed as follows:

1st Row. (This will now be the right side of the work - **rs**)
*K1, p1, repeat from * to last st, k1.

2nd Row. P1, * k1, p1, repeat from * to end.

These 2 rows form 1x1 rib.

Work in 1x1 rib until back measures 6cm, (2½in), finishing after a rs row.

Next Row. P5 **[8:2:8:6:9]**, p2tog, (p**4 [4:5:4:4:4]**, p2tog) **19 [19:19:21:23:23]** times, p6 **[9:2:9:7:10]**.

107 [113:119:123:129:135] sts on the needle

Change to your main needles and work remainder of back as follows:

1st Row. Knit.

2nd Row. Purl.

1st and 2nd rows form stocking stitch.

Working in stocking stitch (throughout) continue until back measures **43 [44:45:46:46:46]**cm, (**17 [17¼: 17¾:18:18:18]**in), finishing after a purl row.

Shape raglan

Cast off **4 [5:5:6:6:6]** sts at beginning of next 2 rows.

99 [103:109:111:117:123] sts on the needle

1st Row. S1, k1, psso, knit to last 2 sts, k2tog.

97 [101:107:109:115:121] sts on the needle

2nd Row. P2tog, purl to last 2 sts, p2togtbl.

95 [99:105:107:113:119] sts on the needle

1st and 2nd rows form raglan shapings.

Work **10 [10:10:12:14:16]** rows decreasing 1 st at each end as before in every row. **

75 [79:85:83:85:87] sts on the needle

Work **42 [46:48:46:46:48]** rows decreasing 1 st at each end as before in 1st and every following alternate row. ***

33 [33:37:37:39:39] sts on the needle

Leave remaining **33 [33:37:37:39:39]** sts on a stitch holder.

Knit the front

Work as given for back to. **

Work **30 [32:34:32:32:34]** rows decreasing 1 st at each end as before in 1st and every following alternate row.

45 [47:51:51:53:53] sts on the needle

Shape neck

Beginning with the rs of the work facing you, divide for the neck as follows:

s1, k1, psso, k**12 [14:14:14:14:14]**, slip remaining **31 [31:35: 35:37:37]** sts onto a stitch holder. You will come back to these **31 [31:35:35:37:37]** sts later to work the second side of neck.

13 [15:15:15:15:15] sts on the needle

Next Row. P2tog, purl to end.

12 [14:14:14:14:14] sts on the needle

Work 2 rows decreasing 1 st at raglan edge as before in 1st row **AT SAME TIME** decreasing 1 st at neck edge in every row.

9 [11:11:11:11:11] sts on the needle

Work **5 [7:7:7:7:7]** rows decreasing 1 st at each end as before in 1st and every following alternate row.

3 sts on the needle

Next Row. Purl.

Next Row. S1, k1, psso, k1.

2 sts on the needle

Next Row. P2tog. Fasten off.

To work the second side of the neck, return the **31 [31: 35:35:37:37]** sts left on a stitch holder onto the main needle. With the right side of the work facing you, slip **17 [15:19:19:21:21]** sts onto a stitch holder, rejoin yarn to remaining **14 [16:16:16:16:16]** sts and knit to last 2 sts, k2tog.

13 [15:15:15:15:15] sts on the needle

Next Row. Purl to last 2 sts, p2tog.

12 [14:14:14:14:14] sts on the needle

Work 2 rows decreasing 1 st at neck edge in every row **AT SAME TIME** decreasing 1 st at raglan edge as before in 1st row.

9 [11:11:11:11:11] sts on the needle

Work 5 [7:7:7:7:7] rows decreasing 1 st at each end as before in 1st and every following alternate row.

3 sts on the needle

Next Row. Purl.

Next Row. K1, k2tog.

2 sts on the needle

Next Row. P2tog. Fasten off.

Knit 2 sleeves, both alike

Using your smaller needles and C, cast on **57** [**57:61:63**:**65:65**] sts. Change to M and proceed as follows:

work in 1x1 rib until sleeve measures 6cm, (2½in), finishing after a rs row.
Next Row. P3 [**3:2:3**:**4:4**], p2tog, (p5 [**5:4:4**:**4:4**], p2tog) 7 [**7:9:9**:**9:9**] times, p3 [**3:3:4**:**5:5**].

49 [49:51:53:55:55] sts on the needle

Change to your main needles and beginning with a knit row work in stocking stitch for the remainder of the sleeve as follows:

work **53** [**47:71:107**:**13:33**] rows increasing 1 st at each end of 5th and every following **6th** [**6th:6th:6th**:**4th:4th**] row (there will be **5** [**5:5:5**:**3:3**] rows straight between each increase row).

67 [65:75:89:61:71] sts on the needle

For 1st, 2nd, 3rd, 5th and 6th sizes only

Work **48** [**56:32:96:78**] rows increasing 1 st at each end of every following **8th** [**8th:8th**:**6th**:**6th**] row (there will be **7** [**7:7**:**5**:**5**] rows straight between each increase row).

79 [79:83:93:97] sts on the needle

For all 6 sizes

Work without further shaping until the sleeve is **47** [**48:48**:**49:50:51**]cm, (**18½** [**19:19:19¼**:**19¾:20**]in), finishing after a purl row.

Shape raglan

Cast off **4** [**5:5:6**:**6:6**] sts at beginning of next 2 rows.

71 [69:73:77:81:85] sts on the needle

1st Row. S1, k1, psso, knit to last 2 sts, k2tog.

69 [67:71:75:79:83] sts on the needle

2nd Row. Purl.

3rd Row. Knit.

4th Row. Purl.

From 1st to 4th row forms raglan shapings.

Work 8 [**20:16:8**:**4:4**] rows decreasing 1 st at each end as before in 1st and every following **4th** [**4th:4th:4th**:**0:0**] row.

65 [57:63:71:77:81] sts on the needle

1st Row. S1, k1, psso, knit to last 2 sts, k2tog.

63 [55:61:69:75:79] sts on the needle

2nd Row. Purl.

1st and 2nd rows form raglan shapings.

Work **40** [**32:38:46**:**52:56**] rows decreasing 1 st at each end as before in 1st and every following alternate row. ******

23 sts on the needle

Leave remaining 23 sts on a stitch holder.

Knit the neckband

Join raglan seams, leaving left back raglan open. With the rs of the work facing you, using your smaller needles and M, work across 23 sts left on a stitch holder at top of left sleeve as follows:

k2, m1, (k6, m1) 3 times, k3, pick up and knit 11 [**13:13**:**13:13:13**] sts evenly along left side of neck, work across **17** [**15:19:19**:**21:21**] sts left a on a stitch holder at front of neck as follows:
k1 [**1:1:1**:**2:2**], m1, (k**7** [**6:8:8**:**4:4**], m1) **2** [**2:2:2**:**4:4**] times, k**2** [**2:2:2**:**3:3**], pick up and knit 11 [**13:13:13**:**13:13**] sts evenly along right side of neck, work across 23 sts left on a stitch holder at top of right sleeve as follows:
k3, m1, (k6, m1) 3 times, k2, work across **33** [**33:37:37**:**39:39**] sts left on a stitch holder at back of neck as follows:
k1 [**1:1:1**:**2:2**], m1, (k**6** [**6:7:7**:**5:5**], m1) **5** [**5:5:5**:**7:7**] times, k**2** [**2:1:1**:**2:2**].

135 [137:145:145:153:153] sts on the needle

Beginning with 2nd row of 1x1 rib work until neckband measures 7cm, (2¾in), finishing after a wrong side row.

Cast off in rib.

To serve

Join left back raglan and neckband seams. Sew side and sleeve seams. Fold neckband in half onto wrong side and slip stitch loosely in position. Pin out garment to the measurements given and cover with damp cloths. See yarn ball band for washing and further care instructions.

Put over head. Add some great company. If made up after 6pm, serve as above, take picture and post to social media showing what you're wearing.
#knitandnibble #lookatme #imadethis

V-neck

Here's how to make it ...

Knit the back

Work as given for back of round neck to. ***

Cast off remaining **33** [**33**:**37**:**37**:39:39] sts.

Knit the front

Work as given for back of round neck to shape raglan.

Shape raglan and divide for neck

Beginning with the rs of the work facing you, divide for the neck as follows:

cast off **4** [**5**:**5**:**6**:6:6] sts, k**46** [**48**:**51**:**52**:55:58], k2tog, turn, slip remaining **54** [**57**:**60**:**62**:65:68] sts onto a stitch holder. You will come back to these **54** [**57**:**60**:**62**:65:68] sts later to work the second side of neck.

48 [50:53:54:57:60] sts on the needle

Next Row. Purl.

1st Row. S1, k1, psso (raglan edge), knit to last 2 sts, k2tog (neck edge).

46 [48:51:52:55:58] sts on the needle

2nd Row. Purl to last 2 sts, p2togtbl.

45 [47:50:51:54:57] sts on the needle

1st and 2nd rows form raglan and neck shapings.

Work **6** [**2**:**8**:**10**:12:8] rows decreasing 1 st at raglan edge as before in every row **AT SAME TIME** decreasing 1 st at neck edge in 1st and every following **2nd** [**0**:**2nd**:**2nd**:2nd:2nd] row.

36 [44:38:36:36:45] sts on the needle

Work **4** [**8**:**2**:**2**:2:8] rows decreasing 1 st at raglan edge as before in every row **AT SAME TIME** decreasing 1 st at neck edge in 1st and every following **0** [**4th**:**0**:**0**:0:4th] row.

31 [34:35:33:33:35] sts on the needle

Work **29** [**33**:**35**:**31**:31:33] rows decreasing 1 st at raglan edge as before in 1st and every following alternate row **AT SAME TIME** decreasing 1 st at neck edge in **1st** [**1st**:**3rd**:**3rd**:3rd:1st] and every following 4th row.

8 [8:8:9:9:9] sts on the needle

Work **11** [**11**:**11**:**13**:13:13] rows decreasing 1 st at raglan edge only as before in 2nd and every following alternate row.

3 sts on the needle

Next Row. S1, k1, psso, k1.

2 sts on the needle

Next Row. P2tog. Fasten off.

To work the second side of the neck return the **54** [**57**:**60**:**62**:65:68] sts left on a stitch holder onto the main needle. With the rs of the work facing you, slip first st onto a stitch marker or safety pin for neckband, rejoin yarn to remaining **53** [**56**:**59**:**61**:64:67] sts and k2tog, knit to end.

52 [55:58:60:63:66] sts on the needle

Next Row. Cast off **4** [**5**:**5**:**6**:6:6] sts, purl to end.

48 [50:53:54:57:60] sts on the needle

1st Row. K2tog (neck edge), knit to last 2 sts, k2tog (raglan edge).

46 [48:51:52:55:58] sts on the needle

2nd Row. P2tog, purl to end.

45 [47:50:51:54:57] sts on the needle

1st and 2nd rows form raglan and neck shapings.

Work **6** [**2**:**8**:**10**:12:8] rows decreasing 1 st at neck edge in 1st and every following **2nd** [**0**:2nd:**2nd**:2nd:2nd] row **AT SAME TIME** decreasing 1 st at raglan edge as before in every row.

36 [44:38:36:36:45] sts on the needle

Work **4** [**8**:**2**:**2**:2:8] rows decreasing 1 st at neck edge in 1st and every following **0** [**4th**:**0**:**0**:0:4th] row **AT SAME TIME** decreasing 1 st at raglan edge as before in every row.

31 [34:35:33:33:35] sts on the needle

Work **29** [**33**:**35**:**31**:31:33] rows decreasing 1 st at neck edge in **1st** [**1st**:**3rd**:**3rd**:3rd:1st] and every following 4th row **AT SAME TIME** decreasing 1 st at raglan edge as before in 1st and every following alternate row.

8 [8:8:9:9:9] sts on the needle

Work **11** [**11**:**11**:**13**:13:13] rows decreasing 1 st at raglan edge only as before in 2nd and every following alternate row.

3 sts on the needle

Next Row. K1, k2tog.

2 sts on the needle

Next Row. P2tog. Fasten off.

Knit 2 sleeves, both alike

Work as given for sleeves of round neck sweater to. **

Cast off remaining 23 sts.

Knit the neckband

Join raglan seams, leaving left back raglan open. With the rs of the work facing you, using your smaller needles and M, pick up and knit 27 sts from 23 cast off sts at top of left sleeve, **52** [**56**:**58**:**58**:60:64] sts evenly along left side of neck, knit 1 st from stitch marker or safety pin at centre of front, pick up and knit **52** [**56**:**58**:**58**:60:64] sts evenly along right side of neck, 27 sts from 23 cast off sts at top of right sleeve and **40** [**40**:**44**:**44**:46:46] sts from **33** [**33**:**37**:**37**:39:39] cast off sts at back of neck.

199 [**207**:**215**:**215**:221:229] sts on the needle

1st Row. (P1, k1) **59** [**61**:**64**:**64**:66:68] times, insert needle purlways through 2nd st and then 1st st and slip both sts off needle together, purl next st then pass 2 slipped sts together over purl st, (k1, p1) **39** [**41**:**42**:**42**:43:45] times.

197 [**205**:**213**:**213**:219:227] sts on the needle

2nd Row. (K1, p1) **38** [**40**:**41**:**41**:42:44] times, k1, insert needle knitways into 2nd st then 1st st and slip both sts off needle together, knit next st then pass 2 slipped sts together over knit st, k1, (p1, k1) **58** [**60**:**63**:**63**:65:67] times.

195 [**203**:**211**:**211**:217:225] sts on the needle

3rd Row. Rib to 3 sts at centre of V, insert needle purlways through 2nd st and then 1st st and slip both sts off needle together, purl next st then pass 2 slipped sts together over purl st, rib to end.

193 [**201**:**209**:**209**:215:223] sts on the needle

4th Row. Rib to 3 sts at centre of V, insert needle knitways into 2nd st then 1st st and slip both sts off needle together, knit next st then pass 2 slipped sts together over knit st, rib to end.

191 [**199**:**207**:**207**:213:221] sts on the needle

Repeat 3rd and 4th row twice more.

183 [**191**:**199**:**199**:205:213] sts on the needle

9th Row. Rib to centre st, m1, p1, m1, rib to end.

185 [**193**:**201**:**201**:207:215] sts on the needle

10th Row. Rib to centre st, m1, k1, m1, rib to end.

187 [**195**:**203**:**203**:209:217] sts on the needle

Repeat 9th and 10th row 3 more times.

199 [**207**:**215**:**215**:221:229] sts on the needle

Cast off in rib.

To serve

Join left back raglan and neckband seams. Sew side and sleeve seams. Fold neckband in half onto wrong side and slip stitch loosely in position. Pin out garment to the measurements given and cover with damp cloths. See yarn ball band for washing and further care instructions.

Put over head. Add some great company. If made up after 6pm, serve as above, take picture and post to social media with choice of drink in hand.

#knitandnibble #lookatme #imadethis

Tone.

Your abs

Your voice

Your sleeves

A casual jumper with different sleeves to body.

Knit in Sublime Extra Fine Merino DK, with a choice of 465 colour combinations.

- Two-tone raglan jumper

Sublime
extra fine merino wool dk

Tone.

Makes: 1 x two-tone jumper in Sublime Extra Fine Merino DK.

7 [**7**:**8**:**8**:**9**:**9**] x 50g balls Sublime Extra Fine Merino DK, main colour shade, **018 - Dusted Grey**

5 [**6**:**6**:**6**:**6**:**7**] x 50g balls Sublime Extra Fine Merino DK, contrast colour shade, **362 - Spruce**

1 x pair of 4mm knitting needles (or the size required to give the correct tension for main knitting)

1 x pair of 3.5mm knitting needles (or a needle 0.5mm smaller than you use for main knitting)

1 x row counter

1 x notepad and pen

1 x measuring tape

4 x stitch holders

1 x scissors

1 x sewing needle

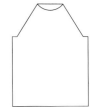

Abbreviations

cm centimetres, **C** contrast, **DK** double knitting, **g** grammes, **in** inch(es), **k** knit, **M** main, **mm** millimetres, **O** no rows, **p** purl, **st(s)** stitch(es), **tbl** through back of loop, **tog** together, **K2tog** insert the right-hand needle through the 2nd and 1st stitches on the left-hand needle and knit them together to form a single stitch, **P2tog** insert the right-hand needle through the 1st and 2nd stitches on the left-hand needle and purl them together to form a single stitch, **P2togtbl** insert the right-hand needle purlways through the back loops of 2nd and 1st stitches on the left-hand needle from left to right and purl them together to form a single stitch, **S1** slip 1 stitch knitways – insert the right-hand needle into next stitch as if to knit but just slip it off the left-hand needle onto the right-hand needle without working, **Psso** pass slipped stitch over – pass the slipped stitch from the right-hand needle over the stitch or stitches you have just worked, **M1** make 1 stitch knitways – pick up loop between last and next stitch and knit into the back of this loop.

Size

To Fit Chest	cm	97	102	107	**112**	117	122
	in	38	40	42	**44**	46	48
Actual Size	cm	97	103	108	**112**	117	123
	in	38	40 ½	40 ½	**44**	46	48 ½
Full Length	cm	68	70	72	**73**	74	75
	in	26 ¾	27 ½	28 ¼	**28 ¾**	29 ¼	29 ½
Sleeve Length	cm	47	48	48	**49**	50	51
	in	18 ½	19	19	**19 ¼**	19 ¾	20

97cm 38in

102cm 40in

107cm 42in

112cm 44in

117cm 46in

122cm 48in

Here's how to make it ...

Check one's tension

With clean hands, cast on **22 sts** and knit **28 rows** in stocking stitch (knit one row, purl one row and repeat) on **4mm** needles or the size required to give correct tension, which should result in a **10cm (4in)** square.

If the square is bigger than this, use a thinner needle, if smaller use a thicker needle.

It's really important to get this bit correct or the jumper will not result in the correct size stated.

Knit the back

Using your smaller needles and M, cast on **127** [**133**:**139**:**145**:153:159] sts.

1st Row. (This will now be the right side of the work - **rs**) * K1, p1, repeat from * to last st, k1.

2nd Row. P1, * k1, p1, repeat from * to end.

These 2 rows form 1x1 rib.

Work in 1x1 rib until back measures 6cm, (2½in), finishing after a rs row.

Next Row. P5 [**8**:**2**:**8**:6:9], p2tog, (p4 [**4**:**5**:**4**:4:4], p2tog) **19** [**19**:**19**:**21**:23:23] times, p6 [**9**:**2**:**9**:7:10].

107 [113:119:123:129:135] sts on the needle

Change to your main needles and work remainder of back as follows:

> **1st Row.** Knit.
> **2nd Row.** Purl.
> 1st and 2nd rows form stocking stitch.

Working in stocking stitch (throughout) continue until back measures **43** [**44**:**45**:**46**:46:46]cm, (**17** [17¼:17¾:**18**:18:18]in), finishing after a purl row.

Shape raglan

Cast off **4** [**5**:**5**:**6**:6:6] sts at beginning of next 2 rows.

99 [103:109:111:117:123] sts on the needle

1st Row. S1, k1, psso, knit to last 2 sts, k2tog.

97 [101:107:109:115:121] sts on the needle

2nd Row. P2tog, purl to last 2 sts, p2togtbl.

95 [99:105:107:113:119] sts on the needle

1st and 2nd rows form raglan shapings.

Work **10** [**10**:**10**:**12**:14:16] rows decreasing 1 st at each end as before in every row. **

75 [79:85:83:85:87] sts on the needle

Work **42** [**46**:**48**:**46**:46:48] rows decreasing 1 st at each end as before in 1st and every following alternate row.

33 [33:37:37:39:39] sts on the needle

Leave remaining **33** [**33**:**37**:**37**:39:39] sts on a stitch holder.

Knit the front

Work as given for back to. **

Work **30** [**32**:**34**:**32**:32:34] rows decreasing 1 st at each end as before in 1st and every following alternate row.

45 [47:51:51:53:53] sts on the needle

Shape neck

Beginning with the rs of the work facing you, divide for the neck as follows:

> s1, k1, psso, k12 [**14**:**14**:**14**:14:14], slip remaining **31** [**31**:**35**:**35**:37:37] sts onto a stitch holder. You will come back to these **31** [**31**:**35**:**35**:37:37] sts later to work the second side of neck.

13 [15:15:15:15:15] sts on the needle

Next Row. P2tog, purl to end.

12 [14:14:14:14:14] sts on the needle

Work 2 rows decreasing 1 st at raglan edge as before in 1st row **AT SAME TIME** decreasing 1 st at neck edge in every row.

9 [11:11:11:11:11] sts on the needle

Work **5** [**7**:**7**:**7**:7:7] rows decreasing 1 st at each end as before in 1st and every following alternate row.

3 sts on the needle

Next Row. Purl.

Next Row. S1, k1, psso, k1.

2 sts on the needle

Next Row. P2tog. Fasten off.

To work the second side of the neck, return the **31** [**31**:**35**:**35**:37:37] sts left on a stitch holder onto the main needle. With the right side of the work facing you, slip **17** [**15**:**19**:**19**:21:21] sts onto a stitch holder, rejoin yarn to remaining **14** [**16**:**16**:**16**:16:16] sts and knit to last 2 sts, k2tog.

13 [15:15:15:15:15] sts on the needle

Next Row. Purl to last 2 sts, p2tog.

12 [14:14:14:14:14] sts on the needle

Work 2 rows decreasing 1 st at neck edge in every row **AT SAME TIME** decreasing 1 st at raglan edge as before in 1st row.

9 [11:11:11:11:11] sts on the needle

Work **5** [**7**:**7**:**7**:**7**:**7**] rows decreasing 1 st at each end as before in 1st and every following alternate row.

3 sts on the needle

Next Row. Purl.

Next Row. K1, k2tog.

2 sts on the needle

Next Row. P2tog. Fasten off.

Knit 2 sleeves, both alike

Using your smaller needles and C, cast on **57** [**57**:**61**:**63**:**65**:**65**] sts.

Work in 1x1 rib until sleeve measures 6cm, (2½in), finishing after a rs row.

Next Row. P3 [**3**:**2**:**3**:**4**:**4**], p2tog, (p5 [**5**:**4**:**4**:**4**:**4**], p2tog) **7** [**7**:**9**:**9**:**9**:**9**] times, p3 [**3**:**3**:**4**:**5**:**5**].

49 [49:51:53:55:55] sts on the needle

Change to your main needles and beginning with a knit row work in stocking stitch for the remainder of the sleeve as follows:

work **53** [**47**:**71**:**107**:**13**:**33**] rows increasing 1 st at each end of 5th and every following **6th** [**6th**:**6th**:**6th**:**4th**:**4th**] row (there will be **5** [**5**:**5**:**5**:**3**:**3**] rows straight between each increase row).

67 [65:75:89:61:71] sts on the needle

For 1st, 2nd, 3rd, 5th and 6th sizes only

Work **48** [**56**:**32**:**96**:**78**] rows increasing 1 st at each end of every following **8th** [**8th**:**8th**:**6th**:**6th**] row (there will be **7** [**7**:**7**:**5**:**5**] rows straight between each increase row).

79 [79:83:93:97] sts on the needle

For all 6 sizes

Work without further shaping until the sleeve is **47** [**48**:**48**:**49**:**50**:**51**]cm, (**18½** [**19**:**19**:**19**¼:**19**¾:**20**]in), finishing after a purl row.

Shape raglan

Cast off **4** [**5**:**5**:**6**:**6**:**6**] sts at beginning of next 2 rows.

71 [69:73:77:81:85] sts on the needle

1st Row. S1, k1, psso, knit to last 2 sts, k2tog.

69 [67:71:75:79:83] sts on the needle

2nd Row. Purl.

3rd Row. Knit.

4th Row. Purl.

From 1st to 4th row forms raglan shapings.

Work **8** [**20**:**16**:**8**:**4**:**4**] rows decreasing 1 st at each end as before in 1st and every following **4th** [**4th**:**4th**:**4th**:**0**:**0**] row.

65 [57:63:71:77:81] sts on the needle

1st Row. S1, k1, psso, knit to last 2 sts, k2tog.

63 [55:61:69:75:79] sts on the needle

2nd Row. Purl.

1st and 2nd rows form raglan shapings.

Work **40** [**32**:**38**:**46**:**52**:**56**] rows decreasing 1 st at each end as before in 1st and every following alternate row.

23 sts on the needle

Leave remaining 23 sts on a stitch holder.

Knit the neckband

Join raglan seams, leaving left back raglan open. With the rs of the work facing you, using your smaller needles and C, work across 23 sts left on a stitch holder at top of left sleeve as follows:

k2, m1, (k6, m1) 3 times, k3, pick up and knit **11** [**13**:**13**:**13**:**13**:**13**] sts evenly along left side of neck, work across **17** [**15**:**19**:**19**:**21**:**21**] sts left on a stitch holder at front of neck as follows:

k**1** [**1**:**1**:**1**:**2**:**2**], m1, (k**7** [**6**:**8**:**8**:**4**:**4**], m1) **2** [**2**:**2**:**2**:**4**:**4**] times, k**2** [**2**:**2**:**2**:**3**:**3**], pick up and knit **11** [**13**:**13**:**13**:**13**:**13**] sts evenly along right side of neck, work across 23 sts left on a stitch holder at top of right sleeve as follows:

k3, m1, (k6, m1) 3 times, k2, work across **33** [**33**:**37**:**37**:**39**:**39**] sts left on a stitch holder at back of neck as follows:

k**1** [**1**:**1**:**1**:**2**:**2**], m1, (k**6** [**6**:**7**:**7**:**5**:**5**], m1) **5** [**5**:**5**:**5**:**7**:**7**] times, k**2** [**2**:**1**:**1**:**2**:**2**].

135 [137:145:145:153:153] sts on the needle

Beginning with 2nd row of 1x1 rib work until neckband measures 7cm, (2¾in), finishing after a wrong side row.

Cast off in rib.

To serve

Join left back raglan and neckband seams. Sew side and sleeve seams. Fold neckband in half onto wrong side and slip stitch loosely in position. Pin out garment to the measurements given and cover with damp cloths until dry.

Place over head and poke arms through. Trousers always help. See yarn ball band for washing and further care instructions.

If made up after 6pm, serve as above, take picture and post to social media showing your 2 tone.

#knitandnibble #2toneme #imadethis

Show.

Show off your knitting

different stitches

a bespoke you

A casual jumper with a choice of round or V-neck, one or two colours, each boasting a garter stitch yolk and a stocking stitch body and arms with set-in sleeves.

Knit in Sublime Extra Fine Merino Worsted, with a choice of 30 colours, if knit in a single colour, or if knit in two colours, a choice of 435 colour combinations.

- 1 x round neck set-in sleeves
- 1 x V-neck set-in sleeves
- 1 x round neck two colour with set-in sleeves
- 1 x V-neck two colour with set-in sleeves

Sublime
THE LUXURY BRAND BY

EXTRA FINE
MERINO WORSTED

Show.

Makes: 1 x garter stitch yoke jumper with set-in sleeves, in one or two colours with a choice of round or V-neck in Sublime Extra Fine Merino Worsted.

Two colour jumper

9 [**9**:**10**:**10**:11:12] x 50g balls Sublime Extra Fine Merino Worsted
main colour shade, **015 - Clipper**

4 [**5**:**5**:**5**:6:6] x 50g balls Sublime Extra Fine Merino Worsted
contrast colour shade, **539 - Charleston**

One colour jumper

13 [**13**:**14**:**15**:16:17] x 50g balls Sublime Extra Fine Merino Worsted,
contrast colour shade, **228 - Roasted Pepper**

Both

1 x pair of 4.5mm knitting needles (or the size required to give the correct tension for main knitting)
1 x pair of 4mm knitting needles (or a needle 0.5mm smaller than you use for main knitting)
1 x row counter
1 x notepad and pen
1 x measuring tape
4 x stitch holders
1 x scissors
1 x sewing needle
1 x stitch marker or safety pin (V-neck only)

Abbreviations

cm centimetres, **C** contrast, **g** grammes, **in** inch(es), **k** knit, **M** main, **mm** millimetres, **O** no rows, **p** purl, **st(s)** stitch(es), **tog** together, **K2tog** insert the right-hand needle through the 2nd and 1st stitches on the left-hand needle and knit them together to form a single stitch, **P2tog** insert the right-hand needle through the 1st and 2nd stitches on the left-hand needle and purl them together to form a single stitch.

Size

To Fit Chest	cm	97	102	107	**112**	117	122
	in	38	40	42	**44**	46	48
Actual Size	cm	99	103	108	**112**	117	123
	in	39	40 ½	42 ½	**44**	46	48 ½
Full Length	cm	68	70	72	**73**	74	75
	in	26 ¾	27 ½	28 ¼	**28 ¾**	29 ¼	29 ½
Sleeve Length	cm	47	48	48	**49**	50	51
	in	18 ½	19	19	**19 ¼**	19 ¾	20

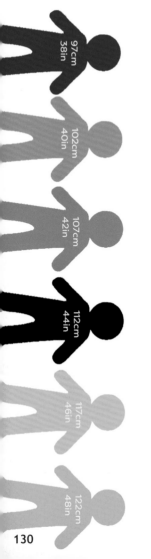

97cm
38in

102cm
40in

107cm
42in

112cm
44in

117cm
46in

122cm
48in

Round neck

Pattern for round neck two colour.

Adjust pattern for one colour option if desired.

Here's how to make it ...

Check one's tension

With clean hands, cast on **18 sts** and knit **24 rows** in stocking stitch (knit one row, purl one row and repeat) on **4.5mm** needles or the size required to give correct tension, which should result in a **10cm (4in)** square.

If the square is bigger than this, use a thinner needle, if smaller use a thicker needle.

It's really important to get this bit correct or the jumper size will not result in the correct size stated.

Knit the back

Using your smaller needles and M, cast on **101 [107:113:117: 123:129]** sts.

1st Row. (This will be the right side of the work – **rs**). * K1, p1, repeat from * to last st, k1.

2nd Row. P1, * k1, p1, repeat from * to end.

These 2 rows form 1x1 rib.

Work in 1x1 rib until rib measures 6cm, (2½in), finishing after a rs row.

Next Row. P5 [7:3:5:1:4], p2tog, (p6 [5:5:5:5:5], p2tog) **11 [13:15:15:17:17]** times, p6 [7:3:5:1:4].

89 [93:97:101:105:111] sts on the needle

Change to your main needles and C (if knitting in two colours), proceed as follows:

starting with a knit row work in stocking stitch until the back measures **40 [41:42:42:42:42]**cm, (**15¾ [16: 16½:16½:16½:16½]**in), finishing after a wrong side row.

Change to your smaller needles and M, proceed as follows:

Next Row. Knit.

This row forms garter stitch.

Work in garter stitch for the remainder of the back as follows:

continue in garter stitch until the back measures **47 [48:49:49:49:49]**cm, (**18½ [19:19¼:19¼:19¼:19¼]**in), finishing after a wrong side row. **

Shape armholes

Work **5 [5:6:6:7:7]** rows decreasing 1 st at each end of every row.

79 [83:85:89:91:97] sts on the needle

Continue without shaping until armholes measure **21 [22: 23:24:25:26]**cm, (**8¼ [8¾:9:9½:9¾:10¼]**in), finishing after a wrong side row.

Shape shoulders

Cast off **13 [14:13:14:14:16]** sts at beginning of next 2 rows.

53 [55:59:61:63:65] sts on the needle

Cast off **13 [14:14:15:15:16]** sts at beginning of next 2 rows. ***

27 [27:31:31:33:33] sts on the needle

Leave remaining **27 [27:31:31:33:33]** sts on a stitch holder.

Knit the front

Work as given for back to **.

Shape armholes

Work **5 [5:6:6:7:7]** rows decreasing 1 st at each end of every row.

79 [83:85:89:91:97] sts on the needle

Continue without shaping until armholes measure **12 [12:13: 14:15:16]**cm, (**4¾ [4¾:5¼:5½:6:6¼]**in), finishing after a wrong side row.

Shape neck

With the right side of the work facing you, divide for the neck as follows:

Next Row. K**34 [36:36:38:38:41]** sts, turn, leave remaining **45 [47:49:51:53:56]** sts onto a stitch holder, you will come back to these **45 [47:49:51:53:56]** sts later to work the second side of the neck.

34 [36:36:38:38:41] sts on the needle

Working on these **34 [36:36:38:38:41]** sts only proceed as follows:

Next Row. Knit.

Work 4 rows decreasing 1 st at neck edge in every row.

30 [32:32:34:34:37] sts on the needle

Work 2 rows decreasing 1 st at neck edge in 1st row.

29 [31:31:33:33:36] sts on the needle

Work **9 [9:13:13:13:13]** rows decreasing 1 st at neck edge in 1st and every following 4th row.

26 [28:27:29:29:32] sts on the needle

Continue without shaping until armhole measures same as back armhole to shoulder shaping, finishing after a wrong side row.

Shape shoulders

Next Row. Cast off **13 [14:13:14:14:16]** sts, knit to end.

13 [14:14:15:15:16] sts on the needle

Next Row. Knit.

Cast off remaining 13 [14:14:**15**:15:16] sts.

To work the second side of the neck return the 45 [47:49:**51**:53:56] sts left on a stitch holder back onto the smaller needles, slip 11 [11:13:**13**:15:15] sts onto a stitch holder, rejoin yarn to remaining 34 [36:36:**38**:38:41] sts and knit to end.

34 [36:36:**38**:38:41] sts on the needle

Next Row. Knit.

Work 4 rows decreasing 1 st at neck edge in every row.

30 [32:32:**34**:34:37] sts on the needle

Work 2 rows decreasing 1 st at neck edge in 1st row.

29 [31:31:**33**:33:36] sts on the needle

Work 9 [9:13:**13**:13:13] rows decreasing 1 st at neck edge in 1st and every following 4th row.

26 [28:27:**29**:29:32] sts on the needle

Continue without shaping until armhole measures same as back armhole to shoulder shaping, finishing after a right side row.

Shape shoulders

Next Row. Cast off 13 [14:13:**14**:14:16] sts, knit to end.

13 [14:14:**15**:15:16] sts on the needle

Next Row. Knit.

Cast off remaining 13 [14:14:**15**:15:16] sts.

Knit two sleeves, both alike

Using your smaller needles and M, cast on 47 [47:49:**49**:53:53] sts.

Work in 1x1 rib for 6cm, (2½in), finishing after a right side row.

Next Row. P1 [1:2:**3**:4:4], p2tog, (p4 [4:4:**6**:4:4], p2tog) 7 [7:7:**5**:7:7] times, p2 [2:3:**4**:5:5].

39 [39:41:**43**:45:45] sts on the needle

Change to your main needles and beginning with a knit row work in stocking stitch for the remainder of the sleeve as follows:

work 53 [41:65:**83**:77:17] rows increasing 1 st at each end of 5th and every following 6th [6th:6th:**6th**:6th:4th] row (there will be 5 [5:5:**5**:5:3] rows straight between each increase row).

57 [53:63:**71**:71:53] sts on the needle

Work 32 [48:24:**8**:16:78] rows increasing 1 st at each end of every following 8th [8th:8th:**8th**:8th:6th] row (there will be 7 [7:7:**7**:7:5] rows straight between each increase row).

65 [65:69:**73**:75:79] sts on the needle

Work without further shaping until sleeve is 47 [48:48:**49**:

50:51]cm, (18½ [19:19:**19¼**:19¾:20]in), finishing after a wrong side row.

Shape sleeve top

Work 5 [5:6:**6**:7:7] rows decreasing 1 st at each end of every row.

55 [55:57:**61**:61:65] sts on the needle

Place marker threads at each end of last row. These 5 [5:6:**6**:7:7] rows will match to 5 [5:6:**6**:7:7] decrease rows on body when sewing the sleeves into armholes.

Work 1 [1:0:**0**:1:1] row more.

Cast off 3 [3:2:**3**:2:3] sts at beginning of next 12 [12:4:**16**:2:14] rows.

19 [19:49:**13**:57:23] sts on the needle

For 1st, 2nd, 3rd, 5th and 6th sizes only

Cast off 4 [4:3:**3**:4] sts at beginning of next 2 [2:12:**14**:2] rows.

11 [11:13:**15**:15] sts on the needle

For all 6 sizes

Cast off remaining 11 [11:13:**13**:15:15] sts.

Knit the neckband

Join right shoulder seam. Using your smaller needles and M, pick up and knit sts around neck as follows:

with right side of the work facing you, pick up and knit 29 [31:31:**31**:31:31] sts evenly down left side of neck, knit across 11 [11:13:**13**:15:15] sts left on a stitch holder at front of neck, pick up and knit 29 [31:31:**31**:31:31] sts evenly up right side of neck and knit across 27 [27:31:**31**:33:33] sts left on a stitch holder at back of neck as follows:
k12 [12:14:**14**:15:15], k2tog, k13 [13:15:**15**:16:16].

95 [99:105:**105**:109:109] sts on the needle

Starting with 2nd row of 1x1 rib work until neckband measures 3cm, (1¼in), finishing after a wrong side row.

Cast off in rib.

To serve

Join left shoulder and neckband seam. Join side and sleeve seams. Sew sleeve tops into armholes matching the 5 [5:6:**6**:7:7] decrease rows on the body to the 5 [5:6:**6**:7:7] decrease rows at the beginning of the sleeve tops.

Pin out garment to the measurements given and cover with damp cloths until dry. See yarn ball band for washing and further care instructions.

Chinos and smart shoes look good with this sweater.

#knitandnibble #largeyolk #imadethis

V-neck

Pattern for V-neck one colour.

Adjust pattern for two colour option if desired.

Here's how to make it ...

Knit the back

Using one colour only work as given for back of round neck sweater to ***.

Cast off remaining **27** [**27**:**31**:**31**:33:33] sts.

Knit the front

Work as given for back to **.

Divide for armholes and neck

Next Row. K2tog (armhole edge), k**42** [**44**:**46**:**48**:50:53], turn, slip remaining **45** [**47**:**49**:**51**:53:56] sts on a stitch holder. You will come back to these **45** [**47**:**49**:**51**:53:56] sts to work the second side of the neck.

Working on these **43** [**45**:**47**:**49**:51:54] sts only proceed as follows:

> **Next Row.** Knit to last 2 sts, k2tog.
>
> 42 [**44**:**46**:**48**:50:53] sts on the needle

Work **3** [**3**:**4**:**4**:5:5] rows decreasing 1 st at armhole edge in every row **AT SAME TIME** decreasing 1 st at neck edge in 1st and every following alternate row.

> 37 [**39**:**40**:**42**:42:45] sts on the needle

Work **3** [**3**:**2**:**2**:1:1] rows more without shaping. Work **12** [**12**:**24**:**24**:24:24] rows decreasing 1 st at neck edge only in 1st and every following 4th row.

> 34 [**36**:**34**:**36**:36:39] sts on the needle

Work **43** [**43**:**37**:**37**:37:37] rows decreasing 1 st at neck edge only in 1st and every following 6th row.

> 26 [**28**:**27**:**29**:29:32] sts on the needle

Continue without shaping until armhole measures same as back armhole to shoulder shaping, finishing after a wrong side row.

Shape shoulders

Next Row. Cast off **13** [**14**:**13**:**14**:14:16] sts, knit to end.

> 13 [**14**:**14**:**15**:15:16] sts on the needle

Next Row. Knit.

Cast off remaining **13** [**14**:**14**:**15**:15:16] sts.

To work the second side of the neck, return the **45** [**47**:49:**51**:53:56] sts left on a stitch holder back onto the smaller needles. With the right side of the work facing you, slip the first st onto a safety pin, knit to the last 2 sts, k2tog (armhole edge).

> 43 [**45**:**47**:**49**:51:54] sts on the needle

Next Row. K2tog, knit to end.

> 42 [**44**:**46**:**48**:50:53] sts on the needle

Work **3** [**3**:**4**:**4**:5:5] rows decreasing 1 st at neck edge in 1st and every following alternate row **AT SAME TIME** decreasing 1 st at armhole edge in every row.

> 37 [**39**:**40**:**42**:42:45] sts on the needle

Work **3** [**3**:**2**:**2**:1:1] rows more without shaping.

Work **12** [12:**24**:**24**:24:24] rows decreasing 1 st at neck edge in 1st and every following 4th row.

> 34 [**36**:**34**:**36**:36:39] sts on the needle

Work **43** [**43**:**37**:**37**:37:37] rows decreasing 1 st at neck edge in 1st and every following 6th row.

> 26 [**28**:**27**:**29**:29:32] sts on the needle

Continue without shaping until armhole measures same as back armhole to shoulder shaping, finishing after a right side row.

Shape shoulder

Next Row. Cast off **13** [**14**:**13**:**14**:14:16] sts, knit to end.

> 13 [**14**:**14**:**15**:15:16] sts on the needle

Next Row. Knit.

Cast off remaining **13** [**14**:**14**:**15**:15:16] sts.

Knit two sleeves, both alike

Work as given for sleeves of round neck sweater.

Knit the neckband

Join right shoulder seam. Then using your smaller needles pick up and knit sts around neck shaping as follows:

> with right side of the work facing you, pick up and knit **62** [**66**:**70**:**72**:74:80] sts evenly down left side of neck, knit stitch left on a stitch marker or safety pin at centre of V, pick up and knit **62** [**66**:**70**:**72**:74:80] sts evenly up right side of neck and **26** [**26**:**30**:**30**:32:32] sts from **27** [**27**:**31**:**31**:33:33] cast off sts at back of neck.
>
> 151 [**159**:**171**:**175**:181:193] sts on the needle

Starting with 2nd row of 1x1 rib proceed as follows:

1st Row. Rib to 3 sts at centre of V, insert needle purlways through back of 2nd st then 1st st and slip both sts off the needle tog, purl next st, then pass 2 slipped sts tog over purl st, rib to end.

149 [**157**:**169**:**173**:179:191] sts on the needle

2nd Row. Rib to 3 sts at centre of V, insert needle knitways into 2nd st then 1st st and slip both sts off the needle tog, knit next st then pass 2 slipped sts tog over knit st, rib to end.

147 [**155**:**167**:**171**:177:189] sts on the needle

Repeat the last 2 rows twice then 1st row once more.

137 [**145**:**157**:**161**:167:179] sts on the needle

Cast off in rib, decreasing 2 sts at centre of V as before.

To serve

Join left shoulder and neckband seam.

Join side and sleeve seams.

Sew sleeve tops into armholes matching the **5** [**5**:**6**:**6**:7:7] decrease rows on the body to the **5** [**5**:**6**:**6**:7:7] decrease rows at the beginning of the sleeve tops.

Pin out garment to the measurements given and cover with damp cloths until dry.

See yarn ball band for washing and further care instructions.

#knitandnibble #knitsirdar #largeyolk #imadethis

Sublime
extra fine merino wool dk

Stripe.

Different colours, one on top of the other

Knit in Sublime Extra Fine Merino DK in a choice of 31 colours

4 examples knit out of a possible choice of 736,281 colour combinations

A band of colour

Now, use your stripes to go faster

- Striped round neck raglan jumper

Stripe.

Makes: 1 x striped jumper in Sublime Extra Fine Merino DK.

50g balls Sublime Extra Fine Merino Wool, as per chart

1 x pair of 4mm knitting needles (or the size required to give the correct tension for main knitting)

1 x pair of 3.5mm knitting needles (or a needle 0.5mm smaller than you use for main knitting)

1 x row counter

1 x notepad and pen

1 x measuring tape

4 x stitch holders

1 x scissors

1 x sewing needle

1 x stitch marker or safety pin (V-neck only)

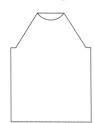

Abbreviations

cm centimetres, **DK** double knitting, **g** grammes, **in** inch(es), **k** knit, **mm** millimetres, **0** no rows, **p** purl, **st(s)** stitch(es), **tbl** through back loop, **tog** together, **K2tog** insert the right-hand needle through the 2nd and 1st stitches on the left-hand needle and knit them together to form a single stitch, **P2tog** insert the right-hand needle through the 1st and 2nd stitches on the left-hand needle and purl them together to form a single stitch, **P2togtbl** insert the right-hand needle purlways through the back loops of 2nd and 1st stitches on the left-hand needle from left to right and purl them together to form a single stitch, **S1** slip 1 stitch knitways – insert the right-hand needle into next stitch as if to knit but just slip it off the left-hand needle onto the right-hand needle without working, **Psso** pass slipped stitch over – pass the slipped stitch from the right-hand needle over the stitch or stitches you have just worked, **M1** make 1 stitch knitways – pick up loop between last and next stitch and knit into the back of this loop.

Size

To Fit Chest	cm	97	102	107	**112**	117	122
	in	38	40	42	**44**	46	48
Actual Size	cm	97	103	108	**112**	117	123
	in	38	40 ½	40 ½	**44**	46	48 ½
Full Length	cm	68	70	72	**73**	74	75
	in	26 ¾	27 ½	28 ¼	**28 ¾**	29 ¼	29 ½
Sleeve Length	cm	47	48	48	**49**	50	51
	in	18 ½	19	19	**19 ¼**	19 ¾	20

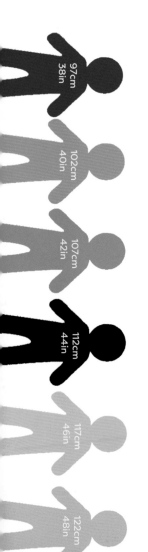

97cm 38in

102cm 40in

107cm 42in

112cm 44in

117cm 46in

122cm 48in

Sweaters as shown from left to right on previous page

Sweater 1

Colour	Shade	Balls of Sublime Extra Fine Merino DK x 50g					
A	364 – Black Cherry	3	3	3	3	4	4
B	578 – Daphne	2	2	2	2	3	3
C	376 – Caramel	2	2	2	2	2	2
D	529 – Eucalyptus	2	2	2	2	2	2
E	483 – Taupe	3	3	3	3	3	4
F	449 – Botanist	3	3	3	3	4	4

Sweater 2

Colour	Shade	Balls of Sublime Extra Fine Merino DK x 50g					
A	409 – Blackcurrant	3	3	3	3	4	4
B	017 – Redcurrant	2	2	2	2	3	3
C	349 – Sunday	2	2	2	2	2	2
D	003 – Alabaster	2	2	2	2	2	2
E	015 – Clipper	3	3	3	3	3	4
F	483 – Taupe	3	3	3	3	4	4

Sweater 3

Colour	Shade	Balls of Sublime Extra Fine Merino DK x 50g					
A	363 – Indigo	3	3	3	3	4	4
B	362 – Spruce	2	2	2	2	3	3
C	361 – Gem	2	2	2	2	2	2
D	489 – Riviera	2	2	2	2	2	2
E	015 – Clipper	3	3	3	3	3	4
F	411 – Pomeroy	3	3	3	3	4	4

Sweater 4

Colour	Shade	Balls of Sublime Extra Fine Merino DK x 50g					
A	409 – Blackcurrant	3	3	3	3	4	4
B	010 – Salty Grey	2	2	2	2	3	3
C	348 – Faye	2	2	2	2	2	2
D	529 – Eucalyptus	2	2	2	2	2	2
E	483 – Taupe	3	3	3	3	3	4
F	375 – Toffee Apple	3	3	3	3	4	4

Stripe Sequence
1 row in B
3 rows in C
2 rows in D
7 rows in E
4 rows in F
6 rows in B
1 row in C
3 rows in D
2 rows in E
7 rows in F
4 rows in A

Here's how to make it …

Check one's tension

With clean hands, cast on **22 sts** and knit **28 rows** in stocking stitch (knit one row, purl one row and repeat) on **4mm** needles or the size required to give correct tension, which should result in a **10cm (4in)** square.

If the square is bigger than this, use a thinner needle, if smaller use a thicker needle.

It's really important to get this bit correct or the jumper size will not result in the correct size stated.

Knit the back

Using your smaller needles and A, cast on **127** [**133**:**139**:**145**:
153:**159**] sts.

1st Row. (This will now be the right side of the work - **rs**) * K1, p1, repeat from * to last st, k1.

2nd Row. P1, * k1, p1, repeat from * to end.

These 2 rows form 1x1 rib.

Work in 1x1 rib until back measures 6cm, (2½in), finishing after a rs row.

Next Row. P**5** [**8**:**2**:**8**:**6**:**9**], p2tog, (p**4** [**4**:**5**:**4**:**4**:**4**], p2tog) **19** [**19**:**19**:**21**:**23**:**23**] times, p**6** [**9**:**2**:**9**:**7**:**10**].

107 [113:119:123:129:135] sts on the needle

Change to your main needles and work in stripe sequence for the remainder of the back as follows:

1st Row. Knit.
2nd Row. Purl.
1st and 2nd rows form stocking stitch.
Working in stocking stitch and stripe sequence (throughout) continue until back measures **43** [**44**:**45**:**46**:**46**:**46**]cm, (**17** [**17¼**:**17¾**:**18**:**18**:**18**]in), finishing after a purl row.

Shape raglan

Cast off **4** [**5**:**5**:**6**:**6**:**6**] sts at beginning of next 2 rows.

99 [103:109:111:117:123] sts on the needle

1st Row. S1, k1, psso, knit to last 2 sts, k2tog.

97 [101:107:109:115:121] sts on the needle

2nd Row. P2tog, purl to last 2 sts, p2togtbl.

95 [99:105:107:113:119] sts on the needle

1st and 2nd rows form raglan shapings.

Work **10** [**10**:**10**:**12**:**14**:**16**] rows decreasing 1 st at each end as before in every row. **

75 [79:85:83:85:87] sts on the needle

Work **42** [**46**:**48**:**46**:**46**:**48**] rows decreasing 1 st at each end as before in 1st and every following alternate row.

33 [33:37:37:39:39] sts on the needle

Leave remaining **33** [**33**:**37**:**37**:**39**:**39**] sts on a stitch holder.

Knit the front

Work as given for back to. **

Work **30** [**32**:**34**:**32**:**32**:**34**] rows decreasing 1 st at each end as before in 1st and every following alternate row.

45 [47:51:51:53:53] sts on the needle

Shape neck

Beginning with the rs of the work facing you, divide for the neck as follows:

s1, k1, psso, k**12** [**14**:**14**:**14**:**14**:**14**], slip remaining **31** [**31**:**35**:**35**:**37**:**37**] sts onto a stitch holder. You will come back to these **31** [**31**:**35**:**35**:**37**:**37**] sts later to work the second side of the neck.

13 [15:15:15:15:15] sts on the needle

Next Row. P2tog, purl to end.

12 [14:14:14:14:14] sts on the needle

Work 2 rows decreasing 1 st at raglan edge as before in 1st row **AT SAME TIME** decreasing 1 st at neck edge in every row.

9 [11:11:11:11:11] sts on the needle

Work **5** [**7**:**7**:**7**:**7**:**7**] rows decreasing 1 st at each end as before in 1st and every following alternate row.

3 sts on the needle

Next Row. Purl.

Next Row. S1, k1, psso, k1.

2 sts on the needle

Next Row. P2tog. Fasten off.

To work the second side of the neck return the **31** [**31**:**35**:
35:**37**:**37**] sts left on a stitch holder onto the main needle. With the right side of the work facing you, slip **17** [**15**:**19**:
19:**21**:**21**] sts onto a stitch holder, rejoin yarn to remaining **14** [**16**:**16**:**16**:**16**:**16**] sts and knit to last 2 sts, k2tog.

13 [15:15:15:15:15] sts on the needle

Next Row. Purl to last 2 sts, p2tog.

12 [14:14:14:14:14] sts on the needle

Work 2 rows decreasing 1 st at neck edge in every row **AT SAME TIME** decreasing 1 st at raglan edge as before in 1st row.

9 [11:11:11:11:11] sts on the needle

Work **5** [**7**:**7**:**7**:**7**:**7**] rows decreasing 1 st at each end as before in 1st and every following alternate row.

3 sts on the needle

Next Row. Purl.

Next Row. K1, k2tog.

2 sts on the needle

Next Row. P2tog. Fasten off.

Knit 2 sleeves, both alike

Using your smaller needles and A, cast on **57** [**57**:**61**:**63**:**65**:**65**] sts.

Work in 1x1 rib until sleeve measures 6cm, (2½in), finishing after a rs row.

Next Row. P3 [**3**:**2**:**3**:**4**:**4**], p2tog, (p5 [**5**:**4**:**4**:**4**:**4**], p2tog) 7 [7:**9**:**9**:**9**:**9**] times, p3 [**3**:**3**:**4**:**5**:**5**].

49 [**49**:**51**:**53**:**55**:**55**] sts on the needle

Change to your main needles and beginning with a knit row work in stocking stitch and stripe sequence for the remainder of the sleeve as follows:

work 53 [**47**:**71**:**107**:**13**:**33**] rows increasing 1 st at each end of 5th and every following 6th [**6th**:**6th**:**6th**:**4th**:**4th**] row (there will be 5 [**5**:**5**:**5**:**3**:**3**] rows straight between each increase row).

67 [**65**:**75**:**89**:**61**:**71**] sts on the needle

For 1st, 2nd, 3rd, 5th and 6th sizes only

Work **48** [**56**:**32**:**96**:**78**] rows increasing 1 st at each end of every following 8th [**8th**:**8th**:**6th**:**6th**] row (there will be 7 [7:7:**5**:**5**] rows straight between each increase row).

79 [**79**:**83**:**93**:**97**] sts on the needle

For all 6 sizes

Work without further shaping until the sleeve is **47** [**48**:**48**:**49**:**50**:**51**]cm, (**18½** [**19**:**19**:**19¼**:**19¾**:**20**]in), finishing after a purl row.

Shape raglan

Cast off **4** [**5**:**5**:**6**:**6**:**6**] sts at beginning of next 2 rows.

71 [**69**:**73**:**77**:**81**:**85**] sts on the needle

1st Row. S1, k1, psso, knit to last 2 sts, k2tog.

69 [**67**:**71**:**75**:**79**:**83**] sts on the needle

2nd Row. Purl.
3rd Row. Knit.
4th Row. Purl.

From 1st to 4th row forms raglan shapings.

Work **8** [**20**:**16**:**8**:**4**:**4**] rows decreasing 1 st at each end as before in 1st and every following 4th [**4th**:**4th**:**4th**:**0**:**0**] row.

65 [**57**:**63**:**71**:**77**:**81**] sts on the needle

1st Row. S1, k1, psso, knit to last 2 sts, k2tog.

63 [**55**:**61**:**69**:**75**:**79**] sts on the needle

2nd Row. Purl.

1st and 2nd rows form raglan shapings.

Work **40** [**32**:**38**:**46**:**52**:**56**] rows decreasing 1 st at each end as before in 1st and every following alternate row. **

23 sts on the needle

Leave remaining 23 sts on a stitch holder.

Knit the neckband

Join raglan seams, leaving left back raglan open. With the rs of the work facing you, using your smaller needles and A, work across 23 sts left on a stitch holder at top of left sleeve as follows:

k2, m1, (k6, m1) 3 times, k3, pick up and knit **11** [**13**:**13**:**13**:**13**:**13**] sts evenly down left side of neck, work across **17** [**15**:**19**:**19**:**21**:**21**] sts left on a stitch holder at front of neck as follows:

k1 [**1**:**1**:**1**:**2**:**2**], m1, (k**7** [**6**:**8**:**8**:**4**:**4**], m1) **2** [**2**:**2**:**2**:**4**:**4**] times, k**2** [**2**:**2**:**2**:**3**:**3**], pick up and knit **11** [**13**:**13**:**13**:**13**:**13**] sts evenly up right side of neck, work across 23 sts left on a stitch holder at top of right sleeve as follows:

k3, m1, (k6, m1) 3 times, k2, work across **33** [**33**:**37**:**37**:**39**:**39**] sts left on a stitch holder at back of neck as follows:

k1 [**1**:**1**:**1**:**2**:**2**], m1, (k**6** [**6**:**7**:**7**:**5**:**5**], m1) **5** [**5**:**5**:**5**:**7**:**7**] times, k**2** [**2**:**1**:**1**:**2**:**2**].

135 [**137**:**145**:**145**:**153**:**153**] sts on the needle

Beginning with 2nd row of 1x1 rib work until neckband measures 3cm, (1¼in), finishing after a wrong side row.

Cast off in rib.

To serve

Join left back raglan and neckband seams. Sew side and sleeve seams. Pin out garment to the measurements given and cover with damp cloths until dry. Place over head and go faster. See yarn ball band for washing and further care instructions. Jeans or chinos look great with this jumper. Wear trainers if you want to go faster.

If made up after 6pm, serve as above, take picture and post to social media with choice of drink in hand.

#knitandnibble #2gofasterstripes #imadethis

Pour.

Into a funnel

A casual jumper with a rolling neckline and embellished with basic stitches

Knit in Sirdar Harrap Tweed DK, with a choice of 12 colours

- Funnel-neck jumper

Pour.

Makes: 1 x funnel-neck jumper in Sirdar Harrap Tweed DK.

9 [**10**:**10**:**11**:**12**:**12**] x 50g balls Sirdar Harrap Tweed shade, **111 - Ackworth**

Oddment of Sublime Extra Fine Merino Worsted, shade **478 - Marmalade**

1 x pair of 4mm knitting needles (or the size required to give the correct tension for main knitting)

1 x pair of 3.5mm knitting needles (or a needle 0.5mm smaller than you use for main knitting)

1 x row counter

1 x notepad and pen

1 x measuring tape

4 x stitch holders

1 x scissors

1 x sewing needle

Abbreviations

cm centimetres, **DK** double knitting, **g** grammes, **in** inch(es), **k** knit, **mm** millimetres, **0** no rows, **p** purl, **st(s)** stitch(es), **tog** together, **K1below** insert right-hand needle into next stitch one row below and knit, **K2tog** insert the right-hand needle through the 2nd and 1st stitches on the left-hand needle and knit them together to form a single stitch, **M1** make one stitch - pick up loop between last and next stitch and work into the back of this loop, **Rib2tog** if the 2nd stitch on left-hand needle is a knit stitch insert the right-hand needle through the 2nd and 1st stitches on left-hand needle and knit them together to form a single stitch, if the 2nd stitch on the left-hand needle is a purl stitch insert the right-hand needle through the 1st and 2nd stitches and purl them together to form a single stitch.

Size

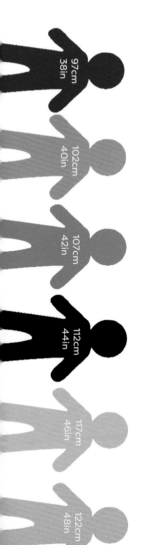

To Fit Chest	cm	97	102	107	112	117	122
	in	38	40	42	44	46	48
Actual Size	cm	97	102	107	112	117	122
	in	38	40	42	44	46	48
Full Length	cm	68	70	72	73	74	75
	in	26 ¾	27 ½	28 ¼	28 ¾	29 ¼	29 ½
Sleeve Length	cm	47	48	48	49	50	51
	in	18 ½	19	19	19 ¼	19 ¾	20

Here's how to make it ...

Check one's tension

With clean hands, cast on **22 sts** and knit **28 rows** in stocking stitch (knit one row, purl one row and repeat) on **4mm** needles or the size required to give correct tension, which should result in a **10cm (4in)** square.

If the square is bigger than this, use a thinner needle, if smaller use a thicker needle.

It's really important to get this bit correct or the jumper size will not result in the correct size stated.

Knit the back

Using your smaller needles cast on **107 [113:117:123:129:135]** sts.

1st Row. (This will be the right side of the work – **rs**). Knit.

This row forms garter stitch.

Work 2 rows more in garter stitch.

4th Row (increase row). K6 [9:6:9:7:10], m1, (k5, m1) **19 [19:21:21:23:23]** times, k6 [9:6:9:7:10].

127 [133:139:145:153:159] sts on the needle

Proceed as follows:

1st Row. * K1, p1, repeat from * to last st, k1.
2nd Row. P1, * k1, p1, repeat from * to end.
These 2 rows form 1x1 rib.
Continue in 1x1 rib until back measures 6cm, (2 ½in), finishing after a right side row.
Next Row. Rib 13 [3:6:4:3:6], rib2tog, (rib **2 [3:3:3:3:3]**, rib2tog) **25 [25:25:27:29:29]** times, rib **12 [3:6:4:3:6]**.

101 [107:113:117:123:129] sts on the needle

Using your main needles proceed as follows:

1st Row. Knit.
2nd Row. Purl.
3rd Row. * K1, p1, repeat from * to last st, k1.
4th Row. P1, * k1below, p1, repeat from * to end.
From 1st to 4th row forms textured rib pattern.
Continue in textured rib pattern until back measures **47 [48:49:49:49:49]**cm, (18 ½ [19:19 ¼:19 ¼:19 ¼:19 ¼]in), finishing after a wrong side row.

Shape armholes

Work 5 [5:6:6:7:7] rows decreasing 1 st at each end of every row.

91 [97:101:105:109:115] sts on the needle

Work on these **91 [97:101:105:109:115]** sts until armholes

measure **11 [11:11:12:12:13]**cm, (4 ¼ [4 ¼:4 ¼:4 ¾:4 ¾:5 ¼]in), finishing after a wrong side row. **

Using your smaller needles proceed as follows:

continue in garter stitch for the remainder of the back until armholes measure **21 [22:23:24:25:26]**cm, (8 ¼ [8 ¾:9:9 ½:9 ¾:10 ¼]in), finishing after a wrong side row.

Shape shoulders

Cast off **13 [15:14:15:16:17]** sts knitways at beginning of next 2 rows.

65 [67:73:75:77:81] sts on the needle

Cast off **14 [15:15:16:16:18]** sts knitways at beginning of next 2 rows.

37 [37:43:43:45:45] sts on the needle

Leave remaining **37 [37:43:43:45:45]** sts on a stitch holder.

Knit the front

Work as given for back to. **

Using your smaller needles proceed as follows:

continue in garter stitch for the remainder of the front until armholes measure **15 [15:16:17:18:19]**cm, (6 [6:6 ¼:6 ½:7:7 ½]in), finishing after a wrong side row.

Shape neck

Next Row. K**38 [41:42:44:45:48]**, turn, leave remaining **53 [56:59:61:64:67]** sts on a stitch holder. You will come back to these **53 [56:59:61:64:67]** sts later to work second side of the neck.

Next Row. Knit.

Work 4 rows decreasing 1 st at neck edge in every row.

34 [37:38:40:41:44] sts on the needle

Work **13 [13:17:17:17:17]** rows decreasing 1 st at neck edge in next and every following alternate row.

27 [30:29:31:32:35] sts on the needle

Continue without further shaping until armhole measures same as back to shoulder, finishing after a wrong side row.

Shape shoulders

Next Row. Cast off **13 [15:14:15:16:17]** sts, knit to end.

14 [15:15:16:16:18] sts on the needle

Next Row. Knit.

Cast off remaining **14 [15:15:16:16:18]** sts.

To work the second side of the neck, return the **53 [56:59:61:64:67]** sts onto the smaller needle. With the right side of the work facing you, slip the first **15 [15:17:17:19:19]** sts onto a stitch holder, rejoin yarn to remaining **38** [**41**:**42**: **44**:45:48] sts and knit to end.

Next Row. Knit.

Work 4 rows decreasing 1 st at neck edge in every row.

34 [**37**:**38**:**40**:41:44] sts on the needle

Work **13** [**13**:**17**:**17**:17:17] rows decreasing 1 st at neck edge in next and every following alternate row.

27 [**30**:**29**:**31**:32:35] sts on the needle

Continue without further shaping until armhole measures same as back to shoulder, finishing after a right side row.

Next Row. Cast off **13** [**15**:**14**:**15**:16:17] sts, knit to end.

14 [**15**:**15**:**16**:16:18] sts on the needle

Next Row. Knit.

Cast off remaining **14** [**15**:**15**:**16**:16:18] sts.

Knit 2 sleeves, both alike

Using your smaller needles cast on **49** [**49**:**51**:**53**:55:55] sts.

Work 3 rows in garter stitch.

4th Row (increase row). K4 [**4**:**5**:**4**:5:5], m1, (k**6** [**6**:**6**:**5**:5:5], m1) **7** [**7**:**7**:**9**:9:9] times, k**3** [**3**:**4**:**4**:5:5].

57 [**57**:**59**:**63**:65:65] sts on the needle

Work in 1x1 rib until sleeve measures 6cm, (2 ½in), ending with a right side row.

Next Row. Rib **3** [**3**:**4**:**4**:5:5], rib2tog, (rib **5** [**5**:**5**:**4**:4:4], rib2tog) **7** [**7**:**7**:**9**:9:9] times, rib **3** [**3**:**4**:**3**:4:4].

49 [**49**:**51**:**53**:55:55] sts on the needle

Change to your main needles and proceed as follows:

1st Row. Knit.
2nd Row. Purl.

1st and 2nd rows form stocking stitch.

Work in stocking stitch for the remainder of the sleeve proceed as follows:

work **51** [**39**:**63**:**105**:111:23] rows increasing 1 st at each end of 3rd and every following **6th** [**6th**:**6th**:**6th**:6th:4th] row (there will be **5** [**5**:**5**:**5**:5:3] rows straight between each increase row).

67 [**63**:**73**:**89**:93:67] sts on the needle

For 1st, 2nd, 3rd and 6th sizes only

Work **48** [**64**:**40**:90] rows increasing 1 st at each end of every following **8th** [**8th**:**8th**:**6th**] row (there will be **7** [**7**:**7**:5] rows straight between each increase row).

79 [**79**:**83**:97] sts on the needle

For all 6 sizes

Continue without further shaping until sleeve is **47** [**48**:**48**: **49**:50:51]cm, (**18 ½** [**19**:**19**:**19 ¼**:19 ¾:20]in), finishing after a wrong side row.

Shape sleeve top

Work **5** [**5**:**6**:**6**:7:7] rows decreasing 1 st at each end of every row.

69 [**69**:**71**:**77**:79:83] sts on the needle

Place a marker at each end of last row.
Work **1** [**1**:**0**:**0**:1:1] rows without shaping.
Cast off **3** [**3**:**2**:**3**:3:3] sts at beginning of next **8** [**8**:**2**:**18**: 16:12] rows.

45 [**45**:**67**:**23**:31:47] sts on the needle

Cast off **4** [**4**:**3**:**4**:4:4] sts at beginning of next **8** [**8**:**18**:**2**:4:8] rows.

13 [**13**:**13**:**15**:15:15] sts on the needle

Cast off remaining **13** [**13**:**13**:**15**:15:15] sts.

Knit the neckband

Join right shoulder seam, then using your smaller needles pick up and knit sts around neck as follows:

with rs facing, starting at top of left shoulder pick up and knit **26** [**28**:**28**:**30**:30:30] sts evenly down left side of neck, knit across **15** [**15**:**17**:**17**:19:19] sts left on a stitch holder at front of neck as follows:
K**7** [**7**:**8**:**8**:9:9], k2tog, k**6** [**6**:**7**:**7**:8:8] at front of neck, **26** [**28**:**28**:**30**:30:30] sts evenly along right side of neck and knit across **37** [**37**:**43**:**43**:45:45] sts left on a stitch holder at back of neck.

103 [**107**:**115**:**119**:123:123] sts on the needle

Starting with 1st row of 1x1 rib work 5 rows in rib.

Change to your main needles and proceed as follows:

starting with a knit row work in stocking stitch until neckband measures 4cm, (1 ½in), finishing after a purl row.

Cast off knitways.

To serve

Join neckband and left shoulder seams. Fold sleeves in half lengthways, then placing folds to seams, sew sleeves in position matching markers on sleeves to decreasing rows on front and back. Join side and sleeve seams. Using oddment of yarn, oversew along outside of seams as illustrated in photograph. Pin out garment to the measurements given and cover with damp cloths until dry. Adorn body with knitted item. See yarn ball band for washing and further care instructions.

#knitandnibble #edging #imadethis

Sublime
extra fine merino wool dk

Calculate.

Because 4x2 = 6
In knitting language it is

A ribbed jumper with folded back neckline for extra cosiness

Knit in Sublime Extra Fine Merino DK, with a choice of 31 colours

• Ribbed jumper

Calculate.

Makes: 1 x ribbed jumper in Sublime Extra Fine Merino DK.

13 [**13**:14:**15**:16:17] x 50g balls Sublime Extra Fine Merino DK shade, **409 - Blackcurrant**

1 x pair of 4mm knitting needles (or the size required to give the correct tension for main knitting)

1 x pair of 3.5mm knitting needles (or a needle 0.5mm smaller than you use for main knitting)

1 x row counter

1 x notepad and pen

1 x measuring tape

4 x stitch holders

1 x scissors

1 x sewing needle

Abbreviations

cm centimetres, **g** grammes, **in** inch(es), **k** knit, **mm** millimetres, **0** no stitches or rows, **p** purl, **patt** pattern, **st(s)** stitch(es), **tog** together, **P2tog** insert the right-hand needle purlways through the 1st and 2nd stitches on the left-hand needle and purl them together to form a single stitch.

Size

To Fit Chest	cm	97	102	107	112	117	122
	in	38	40	42	44	46	48
Actual Size	cm	98	104	109	114	118	124
	in	38 ½	41	43	45	46 ½	48 ¾
Full Length	cm	65	67	69	70	71	73
	in	25 ½	26 ½	27 ¼	27 ½	28	28 ¾
Sleeve Length	cm	47	48	48	49	50	51
	in	18 ½	19	19	19 ¼	19 ¾	20

97cm
38in

102cm
40in

107cm
42in

112cm
44in

117cm
46in

122cm
48in

Here's how to make it ...

Check one's tension

With clean hands, cast on **22 sts** and knit **28 rows** in stocking stitch (knit one row, purl one row and repeat) on **4mm** needles or the size required to give correct tension, which should result in a **10cm (4in)** square.

If the square is bigger than this, use a thinner needle, if smaller use a thicker needle.

It's really important to get this bit correct or the jumper size will not result in the correct size stated.

As long as you knit stocking stitch at the above tension the 4x2 rib should be **22 sts** and **28 rows** to **10cm (4in)** on **3.5mm** needles.

Knit the back

Using your smaller needles cast on **126** [**134**:**142**:**146**:154:**158**] sts.

1st Row. (This will be the right side of the work – **rs**). * K2, p2, repeat from * to last 2 sts, k2.

2nd Row. P2, * k2, p2, repeat from * to end.

These 2 rows form 2x2 rib.

Keeping continuity of 2x2 rib work until rib measures 11cm, (4¼in), finishing after a rs row.

Next Row. P2 [**9**:**7**:**5**:7:**4**], p2tog, (p5 [**4**:**4**:**5**:4:**5**], p2tog) **17** [**19**:**21**:**19**:23:**21**] times, p3 [**9**:**7**:**6**:7:**5**].

> 108 [114:120:**126**:130:136] sts on the needle

Change to your main needles and proceed as follows:

    1st Row. K2 [**5**:**2**:**5**:1:**4**], p2, * k4, p2, repeat from * to last **2** [**5**:**2**:**5**:1:**4**] sts, k2 [**5**:**2**:**5**:1:**4**].
    2nd Row. P2 [**5**:**2**:**5**:1:**4**], k2, * p4, k2, repeat from * to last **2** [**5**:**2**:**5**:1:**4**] sts, p2 [**5**:**2**:**5**:1:**4**].

These 2 rows form 4x2 rib patt.

Continue in 4x2 rib patt until back measures **50** [**51**:**52**:**52**:52:**53**]cm, (**19¾** [**20**:**20½**:**20½**:20½:**21**]in), finishing after a wrong side row.

Shape armholes

Work **5** [**5**:**6**:**6**:7:**7**] rows decreasing 1 st at each end of every row. **

> 98 [104:108:**114**:116:122] sts on the needle

Continue without shaping until armhole measures **21** [**22**:**23**:**24**:25:**26**]cm, (**8¼** [**8¾**:**9**:**9½**:9¾:**10¼**]in), finishing after a wrong side row.

Shape shoulders

Next Row. Cast off **16** [**17**:**17**:**19**:19:**20**] sts in patt at beginning of next 2 rows.

> 66 [70:74:**76**:78:82:] sts on the needle

Next Row. Cast off **16** [**18**:**18**:**19**:19:**21**] sts in patt at beginning of next 2 rows.

> 34 [**34**:**38**:**38**:40:**40**] sts on the needle

Leave remaining **34** [**34**:**38**:**38**:40:**40**] sts on a stitch holder.

Knit the front

Work as given for back to. **

Continue without shaping until armholes measure 12 [12:13: **14**:15:**16**]cm, 4¾ [**4¾**:**5¼**:**5½**:6:**6¼**]in), finishing after a wrong side row.

Shape neck

Next Row. Patt 42 [**45**:**45**:**48**:48:**51**], slip remaining 56 [**59**:63:**66**:68:71] sts onto a stitch holder. You will come back to these 56 [**59**:**63**:**66**:68:71] sts later to work the second side of the neck. Working on these **42** [**45**:**45**:**48**: 48:**51**] sts only proceed as follows:

    Next Row. Patt to end.
    Work 6 rows decreasing 1 st at neck edge in every row.
>   36 [39:39:**42**:42:45] sts on the needle
    Work 4 rows decreasing 1 st at neck edge in 1st and following alternate row.
>   34 [37:37:**40**:40:43] sts on the needle
    Work 5 rows decreasing 1 st at neck edge in 1st and following 4th row.
>   32 [35:35:**38**:38:41] sts on the needle

Continue without shaping until armhole measures same as back armhole to shoulder shaping, finishing after a wrong side row.

Shape shoulders

Next Row. Cast off **16** [**17**:**17**:**19**:19:**20**] sts in patt, patt to end.

> 16 [18:18:**19**:19:21] sts on the needle

Next Row. Patt.

Cast off remaining **16** [**18**:**18**:**19**:19:**21**] sts in patt.

To work the second side of the neck return the **56** [**59**:**63**: **66**:68:71] sts left on a stitch holder back onto the main needles. With the right side of the work facing you, slip **14** [**14**:**18**:**18**:20:20] sts onto a stitch holder, rejoin yarn to remaining **42** [**45**:**45**:**48**:48:51] sts and patt to end.

Next Row. Patt.

Work 6 rows decreasing 1 st at neck edge in every row.

> 36 [39:39:**42**:42:45] sts on the needle

Work 4 rows decreasing 1 st at neck edge in 1st and following alternate row.

34 [37:37:40:40:43] sts on the needle

Work 5 rows decreasing 1 st at neck edge in 1st and following 4th row.

32 [35:35:38:38:41] sts on the needle

Continue without shaping until armhole measures same as back armhole to shoulder shaping, finishing after a right side row.

Next Row. Cast off **16** [**17**:**17**:**19**:19:20] sts in patt, patt to end.

16 [18:18:19:19:21] sts on the needle

Next Row. Patt.

Cast off remaining **16** [**18**:**18**:**19**:19:21] sts in patt.

Knit 2 sleeves, both alike

Using your smaller needles cast on **58** [**58**:**58**:**62**:66:66] sts.

Work in 2x2 rib until sleeve measures 11cm, (4¼in), finishing after a right side row.

Next Row. P5 [**5**:**3**:**3**:5:5], p2tog, (p3 [**3**:**5**:**4**:4:4], p2tog) **9** [**9**:**7**:**9**:9:9] times, p**6** [**6**:**4**:**3**:5:5].

48 [48:50:52:56:56] sts on the needle

Change to your main needles and proceed as follows:

   1st Row. (This will be the right side of the work – **rs**). K2 [**2**:**3**:**4**:0:0], p2, * k4, p2, repeat from * to last **2** [**2**:**3**:**4**: 0:0] sts, k2 [**2**:**3**:**4**:0:0].
   2nd Row. P2 [**2**:**3**:**4**:0:0], k2, * p4, k2, repeat from * to last **2** [**2**:**3**:**4**:0:0] sts, p2 [**2**:**3**:**4**:0:0].

These 2 rows form position of 4x2 rib patt.

Work in 4x2 rib patt for the remainder of the sleeve as follows:

   work **55** [**49**:**73**:**85**:79:17] rows increasing 1 st at each end of 1st and every following **6th** [**6th**:**6th**:**6th**:6th:4th] row (there will be **5** [**5**:**5**:**5**:5:3] rows straight between each increase row).

68 [66:76:82:84:66] sts on the needle

Working increase sts in patt.

Work **48** [**56**:**32**:**24**:32:96] rows increasing 1 st at each end of every following **8th** [**8th**:**8th**:**8th**:8th:6th] row (there will be **7** [**7**:**7**:**7**:7:5] rows straight between each increase row).

80 [80:84:88:92:98] sts on the needle

Working increase sts in patt.

Work without further shaping until the sleeve is 53 [54:54: 55:56:57]cm, (**21** [**21¼**:**21¼**:**21¾**:22:22½]in), finishing after a wrong side row.

Shape sleeve top

Work **5** [**5**:**6**:**6**:7:7] rows decreasing 1 st at each end of every row.

70 [70:72:76:78:84] sts on the needle

Place marker threads at each end of last row. These **5** [**5**:**6**: **6**:7:7] rows will match to 5 [5:6:6:7:7] decrease rows on body when sewing the sleeves into armholes.

Work **1** [**1**:**0**:**0**:1:1] row more.

Cast off **3** [**3**:**2**:**3**:3:3] sts in patt at beginning of next **8** [**8**:**4**: **20**:20:14] rows.

46 [46:64:16:18:42] sts on the needle

For 1st, 2nd, 3rd and 6th sizes only

Cast off **4** [**4**:**3**:**4**] sts in patt at beginning of next **8** [**8**:**16**:6] rows.

14 [14:16:18] sts on the needle

For all 6 sizes

Cast off remaining **14** [**14**:**16**:**16**:18:18] sts in patt.

Knit the neckband

Join right shoulder seam, then using your smaller needles pick up and knit sts around neck as follows:

   with right side of the work facing you, pick up and knit **25** [**27**:**27**:**27**:27:27] sts evenly down left side of neck, knit across **14** [**14**:**18**:**18**:20:20] sts left on a stitch holder at front of neck, pick up and knit **25** [**27**:**27**:**27**:27:27] sts evenly up right side of neck and knit across **34** [**34**:**38**: **38**:40:40] sts left on a stitch holder at back of neck.

98 [102:110:110:114:114] sts on the needle

Starting with 2nd row of 2x2 rib work in rib until neckband measures 6cm, (2½in), finishing after a wrong side row.

Cast off in rib.

To serve

Join left shoulder and neckband seams. Fold neckband in half onto wrong side and slip stitch **loosely** in position. Join side and sleeve seams. Fold rib on back and front in half onto wrong side and slip stitch **loosely** in position. Fold sleeve cuffs in half onto wrong side and slip stitch **loosely** in position. Sew sleeves into armholes matching the **5** [**5**:**6**:**6**:7:7] decrease rows on body to the **5** [**5**:**6**:**6**:7:7] decrease rows marked at the beginning of the sleeve. Pin out garment to measurements given and cover with damp cloths until dry. See yarn ball band for washing and further care instructions. Feel one's algebra become less when this elastic body cover reduces one's hypotenuse.

#knitandnibble #ribbing #imadethis

Walkies.

A man's best friend?

An anagram of the almighty?

Puppy or dog? Perhaps both?

No vet bills, guaranteed.

Insurance optional.

Knit in Sirdar Harrap Tweed DK in a choice of 12 colours.

- Puppy **- doorstop**
- Dog **- draught excluder**

HARRAP TWEED

Walkies.

Makes: 1 x puppy or dog in Sirdar Harrap Tweed DK.

2 x 50g balls Sirdar Harrap Tweed DK:
>   **Puppy** in Sirdar Harrap Tweed DK shade **101 - Gallop**
>   **Dog** in Sirdar Harrap Tweed DK shade **105 - Horbury**

1 x pair of 4mm knitting needles (to check one's tension)

1 x pair of 3.5mm knitting needles (or a needle 0.5mm smaller than you use for main knitting)

1 x row counter

1 x notepad and pen

1 x measuring tape

1 x scissors

1 x sewing needle

2 x buttons for eyes

1 x stitch holder

1 x polyester washable toy filling

1 x a little yarn in different colour for the nose

Abbreviations

cm centimetres, **DK** double knitting, **g** grammes, **in** inch(es), **k** knit, **mm** millimetres, **0** no stitches, times or rows, **p** purl, **patt** pattern, **st(s)** stitch(es), **tog** together, **ws** wrong side, **K2tog** insert the right-hand needle through the 2nd and 1st stitches on the left-hand needle and knit them together to form a single stitch, **P2tog** insert the right-hand needle purlways through the 1st and 2nd stitches on the left hand-needle and purl them together to form a single stitch, **Patt2tog** if the 2nd stitch on the needle is to be 'knit', then k2tog, if it's to be 'purl', then p2tog, **K3tog** insert the right-hand needle through the 3rd, 2nd and 1st stitches on the left-hand needle and knit them together to form a single stitch.

Measurements

	Height		Width		Length	
Puppy	19cm	7½in	10cm	4in	28cm	11in
Dog	21cm	8¼in	13cm	5¼in	32cm	12½cm

Here's how to make it ...

Check one's tension

With clean hands, cast on **22 sts** and knit **28 rows** in stocking stitch (knit one row, purl one row and repeat) on **4mm** needles or the size required to give correct tension, which should result in a **10cm (4in)** square.

If the square is bigger than this, use a thinner needle, if smaller use a thicker needle.

It's really important to get this bit correct or the canine will not result in the sizes stated.

As long as you knit the stocking stitch at the above tension, the ribbed pattern for both the puppy and dog tension should be **22 sts** and **38 rows** to **10cm, (4in)** using **3.5mm** needles.

Knit the tail

Using 3.5mm needles, cast on **12 [13]** sts.

1st Row. (This will be the right side of the work – **rs**). Knit.

2nd to 5th Row. Knit.

6th Row. Purl.

From 1st to 6th row sets ribbed patt.

Working in ribbed patt continue until tail measures 10cm, (4in), finishing after a ws row.

Cast off in patt.

Knit the left side of the body

Worked from tail to nose.

Cast on **28 [31]** sts.

Starting with 1st row of ribbed patt as set for tail, proceed as follows:

1st Row. (Top edge and tail) knit to last **6 [7]** sts (place marker for fold), k**6 [7]**.
2nd Row. Knit.
3rd Row. Increase in 1st st, knit to end.
29 [32] sts on the needle
4th Row. Knit to last 2 sts, increase in next st, k1.
30 [33] sts on the needle

For puppy's body

Work 6 rows in patt increasing 1 st at top edge in 1st and every following alternate row.
33 sts on the needle

For dog's body

Work 5 rows in patt increasing 1 st at top edge in every row.
38 sts on the needle

For both sizes

Work **4 [5]** rows in patt without shaping.

Work **11 [13]** rows in patt decreasing 1 st at top edge in 1st and following **0 [12th]** row.
32 [36] sts on the needle

Next Row. (This will be the wrong side of the work - **ws**).

Cast off **12 [14]** sts for leg, patt to end.
20 [22] sts on the needle

(Place marker for fold and place marker A at end of **12 [14]** cast off sts for leg).

Work **31 [35]** rows decreasing 1 st at top edge in **5th [13th]** row.
19 [21] sts on the needle

(Place marker B at top edge of last row).

Next Row. (This will be the wrong side of the work - ws). Patt to end, cast on **12 [15]** sts for head (top of head).
31 [36] sts on the needle

Work **4 [2]** rows increasing 1 st at top of head in 1st [2nd] and following 2nd [0] row.
33 [37] sts on the needle

Next Row. Patt to end, cast on **12 [14]** sts for leg.
45 [51] sts on the needle

(Place marker C, at beginning of **12 [14]** cast on sts and place marker for fold to correspond with marker on the other leg).

For puppy's body

Work 9 rows increasing 1 st at top of head in 1st and every following 4th row.
48 sts on the needle

For dog's body

Work 6 rows increasing 1 st at top of head in 1st and following 2nd row.
53 sts on the needle

Next Row. Knit to last 2 sts, increase in next st, k1.
54 sts on the needle

For both sizes

Work **12 [14]** rows without shaping.

Next Row. Patt2tog, patt to end.
47 [53] sts on the needle

For puppy's body

Work 2 rows without shaping.

For dog's body

Work 4 rows decreasing 1 st at top of head in 4th row.

52 sts on the needle

For both sizes

Next Row. Cast off **26** [**31**] sts, (place marker D), patt to end. (Place marker for fold to correspond with marker on the other leg).

21 [21] sts on the needle

For puppy's body

Work 8 rows decreasing 1 st at top edge in 1st and every following alternate row **AT SAME TIME** decreasing 1 st at tummy in 1st and following 5th row.

15 sts on the needle

Work 4 rows decreasing 1 st at top edge in 1st row **AT SAME TIME** decreasing 1 st at tummy in 3rd row.

13 sts on the needle

Work 7 rows decreasing 1 st at top edge in 1st and every following alternate row **AT SAME TIME** decreasing 1 st at tummy in 4th row.

8 sts on the needle

For dog's body

Work 6 rows decreasing 1 st at top edge in 1st and following 4th row **AT SAME TIME** decreasing 1 st at tummy in 6th row.

18 sts on the needle

Work 6 rows decreasing 1 st at top edge in 1st and following 4th row **AT SAME TIME** decreasing 1 st at tummy in 6th row.

15 sts on the needle

Work 6 rows decreasing 1 st at top edge in 1st and following 4th row **AT SAME TIME** decreasing 1 st at tummy in 6th row.

12 sts on the needle

Work 5 rows decreasing 1 st at top edge in 1st and following 4th row **AT SAME TIME** decreasing 1 st at tummy in 4th row.

9 sts on the needle

For both sizes

Next Row. Cast off **3** [**4**] sts in patt, patt 4.

5 [5] sts on the needle

Next Row. Patt. (Place a marker at each side of last row).

Cast off remaining **5** [**5**] sts in patt.

Knit the right side of the body

Work from tail to nose.

Cast on **28** [**31**] sts.

Starting with 1st row of ribbed patt as set for tail, proceed as follows:

> **1st Row.** K**6** [**7**], (place marker for fold), knit to end (top edge and tail).
> **2nd Row.** Knit.
> **3rd Row.** Knit to last 2 sts, increase in next st, k1.
> 29 [32] sts on the needle
> **4th Row.** Increase in 1st st, knit to end.
> 30 [33] sts on the needle

For puppy's body

Work 6 rows in patt increasing 1 st at top edge in 1st and every following alternate row.

33 sts on the needle

For dog's body

Work 5 rows in patt increasing 1 st at top edge in every row.

38 sts on the needle

For both sizes

Work **4** [**5**] rows in patt without shaping.

Work **10** [**12**] rows in patt decreasing 1 st at top edge in 1st row.

32 [37] sts on the needle

Next Row. Cast off **12** [**14**] sts for leg, patt to last **0** [**2**] sts, (patt2tog) **0** [**1**] times.

20 [22] sts on the needle

(Place marker for fold and place marker A at end of **12** [**14**] cast off sts).

Work **31** [**35**] rows in patt decreasing 1 st at top edge in **5th** [**14th**] row.

19 [21] sts on the needle

(Place marker B at top edge of last row).

Next Row. Patt to end, cast on **12** [**15**] sts. (Top of head).

31 [36] sts on the needle

For puppy's body

Next Row. Patt.

Work 3 rows increasing 1 st at top of head in 1st and following alternate row.

33 sts on the needle

Next Row. Patt to end, cast on 12 sts.

45 sts on the needle

(Place marker C at beginning of 12 cast on sts and place a marker for fold to correspond with marker on the other leg).

Work 9 rows increasing 1 st at top of head in 1st and every following 4th row.

48 sts on the needle

For dog's body

Work 1 row without shaping.

Next Row. Patt to last 2 sts, increase in next st, k1.

37 sts on the needle

Next Row. Patt to end, cast on 14 sts.

51 sts on the needle

(Place marker C at beginning of 14 cast on sts and place a marker for fold to correspond with marker on the other leg).

Work 6 rows increasing 1 st at top of head in 1st and following 2nd row.

53 sts on the needle

Next Row. Knit to last 2 sts, increase in next st, k1.

54 sts on the needle

For both sizes

Work **12** [**14**] rows without shaping.

Next Row. Patt2tog, patt to end.

47 [53] sts on the needle

Work **2** [**3**] rows without shaping.

For dog's body

Work 1 row decreasing 1 st at top edge.

52 sts on the needle

For both sizes

Next Row. Cast off **26** [**31**] sts (place marker D), patt to end. (Place a marker for fold to correspond with marker on the other leg).

21 [21] sts on the needle

For puppy's body

Work 8 rows decreasing 1 st at tummy in 1st and following 5th row **AT SAME TIME** decreasing 1 st at top edge in 1st and every following alternate row.

15 sts on the needle

Work 4 rows decreasing 1 st at tummy in 4th row **AT SAME TIME** decreasing 1 st at top edge in 1st row.

13 sts on the needle

Work 7 rows decreasing 1 st at tummy in 5th row **AT SAME**

TIME decreasing 1 st at top edge in 1st and every following alternate row.

8 sts on the needle

For dog's body

Work 6 rows decreasing 1 st at top of head in 1st and following 4th row **AT SAME TIME** decreasing 1 st at tummy in 6th row.

18 sts on the needle

Work 6 rows decreasing 1 st at top of head in 1st and following 4th row **AT SAME TIME** decreasing 1 st at tummy in 6th row.

15 sts on the needle

Work 6 rows decreasing 1 st at top of head in 1st and following 4th row **AT SAME TIME** decreasing 1 st at tummy in 6th row.

12 sts on the needle

Work 5 rows decreasing 1 st at top of head in 1st row and following 4th row **AT SAME TIME** decreasing 1 st at tummy in 4th row.

9 sts on the needle

For both sizes

Next Row. Cast off **3** [**4**] sts in patt, patt 4.

5 [5] sts on the needle

Next Row. Patt. (Place a marker at each side of last row).

Cast off remaining 5 sts in patt.

Knit the top of the head

Cast on **6** [**7**] sts for back neck.

Starting with 1st row of ribbed patt as set for tail, proceed as follows:

> **1st Row.** Knit. (Place marker B at each end of row).
> **Next Row.** Knit.
> Work 19 rows in patt, increasing 1 st at each end of 9th and following 10th row.
>
> 10 [11] sts on the needle
>
> Work **8** [**10**] rows increasing 1 st at each end of **8**th [**10**th] row.
>
> 12 [13] sts on the needle
>
> Work **21** [**23**] rows without shaping.

For dog's head

Work 10 rows decreasing 1 st at each end of 1st row.

11 sts on the needle

For both sizes

Work **32** [**24**] rows decreasing 1 st at each end of 1st and every following 8th row. (Top of nose).

4 [5] sts on the needle.

Cast off in patt.

Knit the tummy

Work from side to side.

For puppy's tummy

Cast on 19 sts.

Starting with 1st row of ribbed patt as set for tail, proceed as follows:

1st Row. Knit. (Place markers at end of row for neck edge).
2nd Row. Knit to last 2 sts, increase in next st, k1 (tail edge).

20 sts on the needle

3rd Row. Increase in 1st st, knit to last 2 sts, increase in next st, k1.

22 sts on the needle

4th Row. Knit to end, cast on 13 sts.

35 sts on the needle

5th Row. Increase in 1st st, knit to last 2 sts, increase in next st, k1.

37 sts on the needle

6th Row. Purl to last 2 sts, increase in next st, p1.

38 sts on the needle

7th Row. Increase in 1st st, knit to end, cast on 29 sts.

68 sts on the needle

8th Row. Knit to last 2 sts, increase in next st, k1.

69 sts on the needle

9th Row. Increase in 1st st, knit to end, cast on 4 sts.

74 sts on the needle

10th Row. Knit to last 2 sts, increase in next st, k1.

75 sts on the needle

11th Row. Increase in 1st st, knit to end, cast on 4 sts.

80 sts on the needle

12th Row. Purl to last 2 sts, increase in next st, p1.

81 sts on the needle

13th Row. Increase in 1st st, knit to end, cast on 3 sts.

85 sts on the needle

14th Row. Knit to last 2 sts, increase in next st, k1.

86 sts on the needle

Work 1 row increasing 1 st at tail edge.

87 sts on the needle

Work 2 rows decreasing 1 st at tail edge in every row.

85 sts on the needle

18th Row. Cast off 3 sts, purl to last 2 sts, p2tog.

81 sts on the needle

19th Row. K2tog, knit to end.

80 sts on the needle

20th Row. Cast off 4 sts, knit to last 2 sts, k2tog.

75 sts on the needle

21st Row. K2tog, knit to end.

74 sts on the needle

22nd Row. Cast off 4 sts, knit to last 2 sts, k2tog.

69 sts on the needle

23rd Row. K2tog, knit to end.

68 sts on the needle

24th Row. Cast off 29 sts, purl to last 2 sts, p2tog.

38 sts on the needle

Work 2 rows decreasing 1 st at tail edge in every row **AT SAME TIME** decreasing 1 st at neck edge in 1st row.

35 sts on the needle

Next Row. Cast off 13 sts, knit to last 2 sts, k2tog.

21 sts on the needle

Work 2 rows decreasing 1 st at tail edge in every row **AT SAME TIME** decreasing 1 st at neck edge in 1st row.

18 sts on the needle

Cast off remaining 18 sts in patt.

For dog's tummy

Cast on 22 sts.

Starting with 1st row of ribbed patt as set for tail, proceed as follows:

1st Row. Knit. (Place markers at end of row for neck edge).
2nd Row. Knit to last 2 sts, increase in front, back and front of next st, k1 (tail edge).

24 sts on the needle

3rd Row. Increase in 1st st, knit to last 2 sts, increase in next st, k1.

26 sts on the needle

4th Row. Increase in 1st st, knit to end, cast on 12 sts.

39 sts on the needle

5th Row. Increase in 1st 2 sts, knit to end.

41 sts on the needle

6th Row. Increase in 1st st, purl to last 2 sts, increase in next st, p1.

43 sts on the needle

7th Row. Increase in 1st st, knit to last 2 sts, increase in next st, k1.

45 sts on the needle

8th Row. Increase in 1st st, knit to last 2 sts, increase in next st, k1.

47 sts on the needle

9th Row. Increase in 1st st, knit to end, cast on 29 sts.

77 sts on the needle

10th Row. Knit to last 2 sts, increase in next st, k1.

78 sts on the needle

11th Row. Increase in 1st st, knit to end, cast on 5 sts.

84 sts on the needle

12th Row. Purl to last 2 sts, increase in next st, p1.

85 sts on the needle

13th Row. Increase in 1st st, knit to end, cast on 4 sts.

90 sts on the needle

14th Row. Knit to last 2 sts, increase in next st, k1.

91 sts on the needle

15th Row. Increase in 1st st, knit to end, cast on 4 sts.

96 sts on the needle

16th Row. Knit to last 2 sts, increase in next st, k1.

97 sts on the needle

17th Row. Increase in 1st 2 sts, knit to end.

99 sts on the needle

18th Row. Purl.

19th Row. Knit.

20th Row. Knit to last 3 sts, k3tog.

97 sts on the needle

21st Row. K2tog, knit to end.

96 sts on the needle

22nd Row. Cast off 4 sts, knit to last 2 sts, k2tog.

91 sts on the needle

23rd Row. K2tog, knit to end.

90 sts on the needle

24th Row. Cast off 4 sts, purl to last 2 sts, p2tog.

85 sts on the needle

25th Row. K2tog, knit to end.

84 sts on the needle

26th Row. Cast off 5 sts, knit to last 2 sts, k2tog.

78 sts on the needle

27th Row. K2tog, knit to end.

77 sts on the needle

28th Row. Cast off 29 sts, knit to last 2 sts, k2tog.

47 sts on the needle

Work 3 rows decreasing 1 st at each end in every row.

41 sts on the needle

32nd Row. Knit to last 3 sts, k3tog.

39 sts on the needle

33rd Row. Cast off 12 sts, knit to last 2 sts, k2tog.

26 sts on the needle

Work 1 row decreasing 1 st at each end of 1st row.

24 sts on the needle

35th Row. K3tog, knit to end.

22 sts on the needle

Cast off remaining 22 sts.

Knit 2 ears, both alike

For puppy's ears

Cast on 4 sts.

Starting with 1st row of ribbed patt as given for tail, proceed as follows:

work 5 rows increasing 1 st at each end of every row.

14 sts on the needle

Next Row. Increase in 1st st, patt to end, leave these 15 sts on a stitch holder. Break off yarn.

Cast on 4 sts.

Work 5 rows increasing 1 st at each end of every row.

14 sts on the needle

Next Row. Increase in 1st st, patt to end, patt across **15** sts left on a stitch holder as follows:

patt to last 2 sts, increase in next st, patt 1.

31 sts on the needle

Next Row. Patt.

Work 16 rows decreasing 1 st at each end of 1st and every following alternate row.

15 sts on the needle

Work 2 rows without shaping.

Cast off in patt.

For dog's ears

Cast on 5 sts.

Starting with 1st row of ribbed patt as given for tail, proceed as follows:

work 10 rows increasing 1 st at each end of 1st and every following alternate row.

15 sts on the needle

Leave these 15 sts on a stitch holder. Break off yarn.

Cast on 5 sts.

Work 10 rows increasing 1 st at each end of 1st and every following alternate row.

15 sts on the needle

Next Row. Increase in 1st st, patt to last 2 sts, increase in next st, patt 1, patt across 15 sts left on a stitch holder as follows:

patt to last 2 sts, increase in next st, patt 1.

33 sts on the needle

Next Row. Patt.

Work 6 rows decreasing 1 st at each end of 2nd and every following alternate row.

27 sts on the needle

Work 12 rows decreasing 1 st at each end of 2nd and every following 4th row.

21 sts on the needle

Work 4 rows decreasing 1 st at each end of 2nd and following alternate row.

17 sts on the needle

Work 2 rows without shaping.

Cast off in patt.

To serve

Place left and right sides of body together and sew from tail to marker B at back of neck.

Fold legs in half from markers and sew leg seams.

Sew tummy from tail to back leg, across opening of back leg to marker A then tummy to marker C leaving 8cm (3in), open for stuffing legs, head and body, sew to marker D.

Sew top of head piece from marker B to nose.

Fold ears in half and sew seams. Sew ears to each side of head.

Fold tail in half and stuff lightly. Sew in position.

Using 2 buttons sew them onto face for eyes. Embroider a nose using satin stitch.

Place on parcel shelf of car, or in a dog kennel with head sticking out and cocked to one side.

See yarn ball band and toy filling for washing and further care instructions. Purchase dog basket, feeding bowl, kennel, but never chocolate. It's lethal for dogs and messes up yarn.

#knitandnibble #woof #imadethis

Satin Stitch diagram

163

Play

Games to play when knitting, nibbling or doing both together.

Spider's Web.

Each group receives a ball of Sirdar yarn.

With this they have to tie a strong spider's web, using the legs of furniture.

This should be able to support a 1kg bag of sugar.

Conveyor Belt.

Two pieces of Sirdar yarn about 1-2 metres long are held by two people, one at each end.

A tennis ball is balanced between the 2 lengths of yarn and rolled backwards and forwards from one person to the other without it falling off.

The ball has to touch the hand of the person at each end before it's rolled back along the yarn.

How often can the ball be rolled backwards and forwards this way?

Carry a Mate.

Six to eight people sit on the ground in a circle.

A ball of Sirdar yarn is thrown diagonally backwards and forwards from one person to the next.

Each person that receives the yarn keeps hold of a strand every time they catch it.

Keep going until the ball is finished and a net has been created.

Place a mate on top and see if the weight will support them.

Be kind, don't lift them too high off the floor.

No accidents please.

Conkers.

A classic British game.

Each person takes a conker (a horse chestnut) with a hole made in the middle by using a long nail and a hammer, or a drill.

A length of Sirdar yarn about 30cm (12in) is threaded through the hole with a knot tied at the base of the conker to secure.

A coin is flipped to determine who becomes player 1 or player 2.

The other end is wrapped around player 1's hand with the conker held between two fingers on the other hand, to steady it.

Player 2 dangles their conker by the yarn, while player 1 tries to hit it with their conker.

Player 1 keeps hitting player 2's conker until missed; the players then swap position.

The first player to break the other's conker is the winner.

Nibble

**Something to eat
while knitting.**

Where to Find a Nibble

Use room temperature eggs only please ... and other cooks notes.

Indeed, you can't bake well with cold eggs; your mixture simply won't have the oomph needed to make the cake rise. The human body is like an egg. Both are made of protein. If cold, limbs are not as free to move as when they're warm. It's like jumping into a cold shower. And that's what eggs are like when taken from the fridge. So, if they are at room temperature, they are a lot easier to work with and will hold more air = a better cake.

You see, making cakes is all about the oomph; the air that you capture in the mixture will expand in the oven and allow the cake to rise.

Baking is not that difficult, it's just a matter of care and attention. Just like knitting.

Ensure the following:

- All eggs are medium in size unless otherwise stated

- All spoonfuls and cups are flat, unless otherwise stated

- 1 teaspoon (tsp) = 5ml

- 1 tablespoon (tbsp) = 15ml

- All butter or margarine is unsalted unless specified otherwise

- 1 cup is equivalent to 250g / 250ml / ¼ litre

- For non-fan ovens, increase the temperature by about 20°C / 50°F. It's always best to check with the oven manufacturer's guidelines

- All of the recipes have been tested 3 times, each time using different fan ovens and always baked on the middle shelf

- 180°C = 350°F = Gas Mark 4

- As with any dry-powdered ingredient, it's always best to sieve it first

- A clean metal knitting needle can be used instead of a skewer; 3.5mm is best

Fifteens

Makes 12 slices

15 digestive biscuits (or other sweet-meal biscuits), crushed

15 preserved cherries, drained, cut into quarters

15 marshmallows, cut into quarters

150ml condensed milk

75g (5 tbsp) desiccated coconut

Here's how to make it ...

Place all of the ingredients except for the coconut into a bowl.

Mix together until the mixture becomes a soft, moist dough. If it's a little too dry to the touch, add a drop more condensed milk. Ideally, it should stick to your fingers when lightly touched.

Roll the dough into a long sausage shape about 7cm (3in) thick.

Sprinkle the desiccated coconut over the sausage-shaped mixture. Pat it all over with your hands and wrap in food wrap.

Place in the fridge to set for 2–3 hours.

Cut into 12 even slices with a knife.

Nibble.

Chocolate and Raspberry Slice

Makes 8 slices

Ganache
500ml whipping cream
500g chocolate, chopped
60g butter, cut into small pieces, softened

Mascarpone cream
3 sheets of gelatine, soaked in 4 tbsp cream
250g mascarpone
100ml cream, less 4 tbsp to soak gelatine
Zest of 1 lemon, finely grated
50g icing sugar

To serve
Fresh raspberries
Icing sugar, to dredge

Here's how to make it ...

Prepare a baking tray 18 x 30cm (7 x 12in) by lining with food wrap.

To make the ganache: bring the cream to the boil in a large pan. Remove from the heat and pour over the chocolate, stirring until melted and is fully incorporated into the cream. Stir in the butter. Pour into prepared baking tray, cover and refrigerate until set.

To make the mascarpone cream: warm the 4 tbsp cream and add the gelatine. Set aside to melt.

Whip the mascarpone and cream together until fluffy. Add the lemon zest, icing sugar and gelatine; fold thoroughly.

Spread the mascarpone mixture evenly across the ganache, cover and refrigerate for 2-3 hours until set.

When set, remove the cover, turn upside down onto a flat surface and slice into 8 rectangles with a warm knife.

Decorate with fresh raspberries and icing sugar.

Nibble.

White Chocolate and Coconut Snowballs

Makes 30 snowballs

300g white chocolate
50g butter or margarine
1 ready-made Madeira cake
125g desiccated coconut

Here's how to make it ...

Break half of the chocolate into small squares and place in a bowl over a pan of simmering water with the butter. Allow to melt.

Place the Madeira cake into a food processor, whizz until crumbs.

Mix the cake and chocolate mixture together.

When cool enough to handle, take small pieces and roll between the palms of your hands to form balls. Place onto a tray and chill for 1 hour.

Melt the remaining chocolate in a bowl over a pan of simmering water.

Cover the snowballs in the melted chocolate and desiccated coconut. Chill for 1 hour.

Nibble.

Granola Bars

Makes 10 bars

220g dates, pitted, soaked in boiling water for 10 minutes
85g maple syrup or honey
65g peanut butter
120g roasted almonds, roughly chopped
150g rolled oats
120g dried fruit

Here's how to make it ...

Line a baking tray 20 x 20cm (8 x 8in) with baking parchment.

Drain the dates and whizz in a food processor until soft.

Over a low heat, warm the maple syrup or honey and peanut butter in a pan to soften.

Place all remaining ingredients into a large mixing bowl and mix thoroughly. Pour in the date and peanut butter mix. Stir to combine.

Pour mixture into the baking tray, smooth over and place in the fridge until set.

Cut into 10 bars.

Nibble.

Mars Krispies

Makes 10 squares

3 Mars Bars, cut into slices
50g butter or margarine
90g Rice Krispies or puffed rice cereal
200g milk chocolate, melted, to cover

Here's how to make it ...

Place the Mars Bar slices and the butter or margarine into a bowl set over a pan of simmering water. Stir until all melted.

Stir through the Rice Krispies.

Place into a greased baking tray 18 x 30cm (7 x 12in).

Allow to cool for 20 minutes before covering with the melted milk chocolate.

Cut into 10 squares.

Nibble.

Cake in a Cup

Makes 1 cake

25g butter or margarine, softened
25g caster sugar
½ egg
25g self-raising flour
Spoonful of jam

Here's how to make it ...

Cream the butter or margarine and sugar together until light and fluffy.

Add the egg and beat well, then add the flour and mix thoroughly.

Place the jam in the base of a microwave-safe cup or mug. Spoon the cake mixture on top.

Microwave on high for 2½ minutes (based on a category E microwave).

Nibble.

Nectarine Cake

Makes 10 slices

500g nectarines, cut into eighths
20g caster sugar
225g self-raising flour
1 tsp baking powder
200g butter or margarine, softened
90g caster sugar
2 eggs, beaten
Freshly grated zest and juice of 1 orange
125ml milk

Here's how to make it ...

Preheat the oven to 180°C / 350°F / Gas Mark 4. Grease and line with baking parchment a 23cm (9½in) round cake tin.

Place the nectarines into a bowl and sprinkle with the 20g of caster sugar. Set aside.

Sift the flour and baking powder together. Set aside.

Cream the butter or margarine and sugar together until light and fluffy. The mixture should fall off a spoon to the count of two.

Gradually add the eggs to the butter and sugar, a third at a time until combined. Add the orange zest and juice.

Add a third of the flour, mix into the mixture, then add a third of the milk, mix thoroughly and repeat until all combined.

Place the mixture into the cake tin with the nectarines on top.

Bake for 1 hour until the cake comes away from the sides of the tin and a skewer comes out clean when inserted into the middle of the cake. Allow to stand for 15 minutes before turning out onto a cooling tray.

Cut into 10 slices.

Nibble.

Apple Traybake

Makes 10 slices

450g cooking apples, peeled cored and thinly sliced
Juice of ½ lemon
225g butter or margarine, softened
280g golden caster sugar
4 eggs
2 tsp vanilla extract
350g self-raising flour
2 tsp baking powder
Demerara sugar to sprinkle

Here's how to make it ...

Preheat the oven to 180°C / 350°F / Gas Mark 4.

Grease and line with baking parchment a rectangular baking tray approximately 18 x 30cm (7 x 12in).

Sprinkle the apples with the lemon juice.

Place all the remaining ingredients (except the demerara sugar) into a bowl and mix well with a wooden spoon until smooth.

Spread half of the mixture into the prepared baking tray. Arrange half of the apples on top of the mixture, and then repeat the layers.

Sprinkle with the demerara sugar and bake for 45-50 minutes until golden and springy to the touch.

Leave to cool for 10 minutes before turning the cake out. Remove the paper and cut into slices.

Nibble.

Malteser Squares

Makes 10 squares

100g butter
200g milk chocolate
3 tbsp golden syrup
225g digestive or other sweet-meal biscuits, crushed
225g Maltesers
100g white chocolate, melted

Here's how to make it ...

Melt the butter, milk chocolate and golden syrup in a bowl over a pan of simmering water.

Add the crushed biscuits and Maltesers.

Mix together quickly and pour into a lined baking tray 18 x 30cm (7 x 12in) and chill until set.

Drizzle the melted white chocolate over the top. Allow to set for 1½ hours.

Cut into 10 squares.

Nibble.

Eton Mess Cake

Makes 10 slices

175g butter or margarine
5 tbsp double cream from a 300ml pot
1 tsp vanilla extract
225g plain flour
100g ground almonds
1 tsp baking powder
200g caster sugar
5 egg whites
400g strawberries, sliced
150g meringues, roughly broken
Icing sugar for dusting

Here's how to make it ...

Grease and line with baking parchment a deep baking tray 20 x 30cm (8 x 12in). Preheat the oven to 180°C / 350°F / Gas Mark 4.

Melt the butter and remove from the heat. Stir in the double cream and vanilla extract.

Mix the flour, almonds and baking powder together and set aside.

Place the caster sugar and egg whites into a bowl, whisk to soft peaks.

Add the butter/cream mixture to the flour mixture and stir thoroughly.

Taking a spoonful at a time, gently fold in the egg whites. Fold in half of the strawberries.

Bake for 40-45 minutes until risen, golden, and slightly springy to the touch. Allow to cool.

To serve: whip the remaining cream and spread on top of the cake. Place strawberries and broken meringues on top, dust with icing sugar.

Cut into 10 slices.

Nibble.

Marmalade Cake

Makes 8 slices

200g self-raising flour

100g butter or margarine, softened

2 eggs, beaten

75g caster sugar

2 large tbsp orange marmalade

1 tsp finely grated orange zest

2 tbsp milk

Here's how to make it ...

Preheat the oven to 180˚C / 350°F / Gas Mark 4.

Grease and line with baking parchment an 18cm (7in) round cake tin.

Place the flour into a bowl and rub in the butter or margarine until the mixture resembles fine breadcrumbs.

Stir in all the other ingredients until the mixture is like a thick batter.

Pour into the cake tin and bake for 1 hour until the cake is risen and golden in colour.

Allow to cool for 10 minutes, turn the cake out onto a cooling rack.

Cut into 8 slices.

Nibble.

Sticky Toffee Bars

Makes 16 bars

4 tbsp ready-made caramel

175g butter or margarine, softened

150g light Muscovado sugar

175g self-raising flour

½ tsp baking powder

2 tbsp ground almonds

3 eggs

<u>Toffee icing</u>

150g butter or margarine, softened

200g icing sugar

4 tbsp ready-made caramel

Large pinch sea salt

Here's how to make it ...

Preheat the oven to 180°C / 350°F / Gas Mark 4.

Line a 23cm (9in) square tin with baking parchment and spread the caramel over the base.

Place all the other ingredients into a bowl and whisk until smooth. Pour over the caramel base.

Bake for 30 minutes until golden and springy to the touch.

Cool in the tin for 5 minutes and turn upside down onto a cooling rack. Remove the paper, scraping off any caramel stuck to it, and spreading back onto the cake.

To make the toffee icing: whisk the butter or margarine and icing sugar together until light and fluffy.

Add the caramel and salt, whisk thoroughly. Spread on top of the cake.

Cut into 16 bars.

Nibble.

Chilli Mocha Slice

Makes 10 slices

225g butter or margarine, softened
100g caster sugar
300g plain flour
40g cornflour

Filling

200g plain chocolate
100g butter or margarine
1 tbsp coffee, dissolved in 1 tbsp water
1 tsp mild chilli powder
1–2 tsp ground cinnamon
150ml sour cream
175g dark Muscovado sugar
3 eggs, beaten

Here's how to make it ...

Preheat the oven to 180°C / 350°F / Gas Mark 4.

To make the base, cream butter or margarine and sugar together until light and fluffy. The mixture should fall off a spoon to the count of two.

Add both flours and mix thoroughly.

Spread evenly onto the base of a 23cm (9in) square baking tray.

Bake for 10 minutes.

To make the filling: put all the ingredients (except the eggs) in a bowl over a pan of simmering water to melt.

Gradually beat in the eggs.

Pour over the base and bake for 25 minutes.

Remove from the oven and leave to cool for 15 minutes before serving.

Cut into 10 slices.

Nibble.

Melting Moments

Makes 20

50g caster sugar
50g butter or margarine, softened
75g self-raising flour
Chocolate drops / buttons

Here's how to make it ...

Preheat the oven to 180°C / 350°F / Gas Mark 4.

Grease and line with baking parchment 2 or 3 baking trays, depending on their size.

Cream the butter or margarine and caster sugar until light and fluffy.

Add the flour and knead to make a dough.

Divide into 20 even-sized pieces.

With wet hands, roll each piece into a ball.

Place each ball onto a baking tray and with your finger, press gently in the centre. Place a chocolate drop where the finger hole is.

Bake for 15 minutes until golden and allow to cool.

Nibble.

Caramel Nut Cake

Makes 8 slices

Caramel
80g soft brown sugar
3 tbsp hot water

Fudge Icing
300g soft brown sugar
125ml milk
25g butter or margarine
½ tsp vanilla extract

Cake
150g butter or margarine, softened
250g caster sugar
½ tsp vanilla extract
3 eggs
300g self-raising flour
1½ tsp baking powder
Pinch of salt
300ml milk
125g pecans, chopped

Here's how to make it ...

Preheat the oven to 180°C / 350°F / Gas Mark 4.

Grease and line with baking parchment a 23cm (9in) round cake tin.

To make the caramel: heat the brown sugar in a saucepan until melted. Stir in the hot water carefully. Set aside to cool.

To make the cake: cream the butter or margarine and sugar together until light and fluffy. Add vanilla extract and beat in the eggs. Add the cooled caramel and again, gradually, beat into the mixture.

Add the flour, baking powder, salt and milk. Mix thoroughly and then fold in the pecans.

Bake for 1½ hours until the cake comes away from the sides of the cake tin and a skewer comes out clean when inserted. Remove from the oven and turn out onto a cooling rack.

To make the icing: place the soft brown sugar, milk and butter or margarine into a saucepan and heat gently until sugar has dissolved. Bring to the boil, stirring continuously; boil until a little amount forms a soft ball when dropped in cold water. Remove from the heat, add the vanilla extract and beat until the mixture thickens.

Cover the cake with the icing as quickly as possible. Allow to set for approx. 30 minutes and cut into 8 slices.

Nibble.

Pineapple Squares

Makes 10 squares

1 packet digestive (or other sweet-meal) biscuits, crushed, reserving 2-3 tbsp
100g butter or margarine, melted
75g butter or margarine, softened
200g icing sugar
200ml fresh whipping cream
200g tin of crushed pineapple, drained

Here's how to make it ...

Mix the crushed biscuits with 100g of the melted butter or margarine. Press into a baking tray 20cm (8in) square and leave in the fridge overnight to set.

Beat the icing sugar and the softened butter or margarine until light and fluffy. Spoon over the biscuit base and return to the fridge for 2 hours.

Beat the fresh whipping cream until stiff and then gently fold in the pineapple. Spread evenly on top of the butter and sugar mixture.

Sprinkle some crushed biscuits over the top.

Chill for a few hours.

Cut into 10 squares.

Nibble.

Gingery Plum Cake

Makes 8 slices

Butter for greasing
2 tbsp demerara sugar
500g plums, cut in half and stoned
175g butter or margarine
175g dark Muscavado sugar
140g golden or maple syrup
2 eggs, lightly beaten
200ml milk
300g self-raising flour
½ tsp bicarbonate of soda
1 tbsp ground ginger
1 tsp mixed spice

Here's how to make it ...

Preheat the oven to 180°C / 350°F / Gas Mark 4.

Grease and line with baking parchment a round 23cm (9in) cake tin. Butter the top of the paper. Sprinkle the demerara sugar over the butter and place the plums, cut side down, on top of the sugar.

To make the cake: melt the butter or margarine, sugar and syrup in a large pan over a low heat, stirring until smooth. Remove from the heat and allow to cool for 10 minutes.

Stir in the eggs and milk.

Sift in the flour, bicarbonate of soda and spices. Mix to a smooth batter.

Pour the mixture over the plums and bake for 45-55 minutes until firm to the touch. Allow to stand in the tin for 10 minutes before turning onto a wire rack to cool.

Cut into 8 slices.

Nibble.

Apricot Shortbread

Makes 16 squares

200g dried apricots, finely chopped

5 tbsp apricot jam

4 tbsp water

250g butter or margarine

100g caster sugar and some extra for sprinkling

1 tsp vanilla extract

250g plain flour

140g rice flour

Caster sugar for dredging

Here's how to make it ...

Preheat the oven to 180°C / 350°F / Gas Mark 4.

Grease and line with baking parchment a 23cm (9in) square cake tin.

Place the apricots, jam and water into a small pan. Simmer for a few minutes until thickened and then gently mash with a fork. Allow to cool.

Whisk the butter or margarine, caster sugar and vanilla extract together until light and fluffy. Add both flours and mix with a wooden spoon to form a dough. Divide into 2 pieces.

Lay one piece of dough in the cake tin and spread the apricot mixture on top.

Roll the other piece of dough on a lightly floured surface to the size of the tin and place on top. Prick all over with a fork.

Bake for 25-30 minutes until the edges start to golden.

Remove from the oven and leave to cool in the tin.

Sprinkle with the extra caster sugar and cut into 16 squares.

Nibble.

Meringues Rumtopf

Makes 6 slices

6 egg whites
Pinch of salt
350g caster sugar, sieved
½ tsp vanilla extract
1 tbsp white wine vinegar
1 tsp cornflour
300ml double cream, whipped
Rumtopf (which literally means rum pot, is a German preserved fruit dessert, traditionally eaten around Christmas)

Here's how to make it ...

Preheat the oven to 110°C / 220°F / Gas Mark ¼.

Place the egg whites into a clean grease free bowl and whisk to form soft peaks.

With the mixer on full power, pour in the caster sugar in a steady stream. The mixture will go shiny and form stiff peaks when the whisk attachment is removed. Now add the vanilla extract, white wine vinegar and cornflour. Mix on full power for a few more seconds.

Draw 6 circles on a piece of baking parchment using the base of a mug as a guide. Turn the paper upside down (non-shiny side up) and spread the mixture to the edges of each circle.

Place the meringues in the oven for 2–3 hours until crisp and dried out.

Gently remove the meringues from the baking parchment and place on a wire rack to cool.

Decorate with whipped cream and serve with Rumtopf.

Nibble.

Lemon Drizzle Slices

Makes 10 slices

70g butter or margarine, softened

120g caster sugar

2 eggs

140g self-raising flour

1 tsp baking powder

Freshly grated zest of 1 lemon

1 tbsp lemon curd

2 tbsp milk

Topping

30g granulated sugar

Freshly squeezed juice of 1 lemon

150g icing sugar

2-3 tbsp water

Here's how to make it ...

Preheat the oven to 180°C / 350°F/ Gas Mark 4.

Grease and line with baking parchment a 20 x 20cm (8 x 8in) square cake tin.

Beat the butter or margarine and sugar together until light and fluffy.

Add the eggs and beat again, and don't worry if it curdles. Add all the other ingredients and mix with a wooden spoon until combined.

Pour the mixture into the cake tin and bake for 25-30 minutes until golden and the edges have come away from the sides of the cake tin.

Make some holes in the top of the cake as soon as it comes out of the oven with a skewer, or knitting needle.

Mix the granulated sugar and lemon juice together, pour over the cake.

Mix the icing sugar with water and drizzle over the top.

Cut into 10 slices.

Nibble.

Sweetie Rocky Road

Makes 8 bars

100g butter or margarine, plus extra for greasing
200g dark chocolate, broken into pieces
3 tbsp golden syrup
225g digestive (or other sweet-meal biscuits), crushed
100g small jelly sweets
100g M&Ms

For Decorating
50g dark chocolate, melted
100g small jelly sweets
100g M&Ms

Here's how to make it ...

Grease and line with baking parchment a baking tray 18 x 30cm (7 x 12in).

Put the butter or margarine, chocolate and golden syrup in a large bowl and melt over a pan of simmering water.

Add all the remaining ingredients and pour into prepared baking tray.

Cover and place in the fridge for 20 minutes to set.

Cover with the remaining chocolate and decorate with sweets.

Leave to set and cut into 8 bars.

Nibble.

Nutty Florentine Bars

Makes 8 bars

225g salted butter

175g caster sugar

2 drops almond extract

200g plain flour, plus 1 extra tbsp

100g rice flour

75ml double cream

50g toasted flaked almonds

25g each of whole blanched almonds, walnuts, pecans and hazelnuts, roughly chopped

50g glacé cherries, chopped

25g dried cherries

50g dark chocolate, melted

Here's how to make it ...

Preheat the oven to 180°C / 350°F / Gas Mark 4.

Line a 20cm (8in) square cake tin with parchment paper.

Cream 200g of the butter and 100g of the sugar until light and fluffy. Add the almond extract, plain flour and rice flour, mix to form a dough. Press into the base of the cake tin, cover and chill for 30 minutes.

Remove the base from the fridge, uncover, prick all over with a fork and bake for 25 minutes.

Over a medium heat, melt the remaining butter and sugar and the extra tbsp of flour. Once the butter has melted, add all the nuts and both cherries. Dot this mixture over the baked base, flatten with a spoon and return to the oven for 10-15 minutes until golden.

Once cool, drizzle with the melted dark chocolate and cut into 8 bars.

Nibble.

Peach Melba Squares

Makes 10 squares

250g butter or margarine

300g caster sugar

1 tsp vanilla extract

3 large eggs

200g self-raising flour

100g ground almonds

2 ripe peaches, stoned, halved and each half cut into 4 slices

100g raspberries

1 tbsp flaked almonds

Icing sugar for dusting

Here's how to make it ...

Preheat the oven to 180°C / 350°F / Gas Mark 4.

Grease and line with baking parchment a baking tray 18 x 30cm (7 x 12in).

Gently melt the butter or margarine in a large pan. Remove from the heat to cool for a few moments and then add the sugar, vanilla and eggs. Beat until smooth with a wooden spoon. Stir in the self-raising flour and ground almonds.

Pour the mixture into the prepared tin and lay the peach slices evenly on top. Scatter with the raspberries and flaked almonds.

Bake for 1 hour, covering with foil after 40 minutes. Make sure it's cooked in the middle.

Remove from the oven and allow to cool for 20 minutes in the tin with the foil removed.

Dust with icing sugar and cut into 10 squares.

Nibble.

Marshmallow Delights

Makes 10 squares

50g butter or margarine
½ tin condensed milk
240g digestive biscuits (or other sweet-meal biscuits), crushed, reserving 2 tbsp
200g marshmallows, cut in half
100g desiccated coconut
200g white chocolate, melted

Here's how to make it ...

Put the butter or margarine and condensed milk in a saucepan. Warm over a gentle heat until the butter or margarine has melted.

Remove from the heat and add the crushed biscuits, marshmallows and desiccated coconut.

Mix well and place into a baking tray 18 x 30cm (7 x 12in).

Press the mixture firmly into the tray using your (clean) fingertips.

Cover immediately with the melted white chocolate, sprinkle with the reserved crushed digestive biscuits and refrigerate.

Cut into 10 squares when cold.

Nibble.

Rolled Oats Shortbread

Makes 10 shortbreads

350g butter or margarine
175g caster sugar
175g plain flour
100g desiccated coconut
400g rolled porridge oats
Caster sugar for sprinkling

Here's how to make it ...

Preheat the oven to 180°C / 350°F / Gas Mark 4.

Cream the butter or margarine and sugar until light and fluffy.

Stir in the plain flour.

Mix in the desiccated coconut and rolled porridge oats.

Roll out on a floured board and cut into rounds using a scone cutter. Place on a baking tray.

Bake for 20 minutes.

When cooked, sprinkle with sugar while still warm.

Nibble.

Black Forest Brownies

Makes 10 brownies

200g butter, plus extra for greasing

225g light soft brown sugar

200g caster sugar

125g cocoa powder

100g dark chocolate, broken into chunks

Pinch of sea salt

4 tbsp kirsch or cherry liqueur

4 eggs, lightly beaten

125g self-raising flour

200g fresh, or preserved cherries, stoned, chopped and drained

300ml whipping cream

1 tbsp kirsch

3 tbsp icing sugar

To finish

Icing sugar

Cocoa powder

Fresh cherries

Here's how to make it ...

Preheat the oven to 180°C / 350°F / Gas Mark 4.

Grease and line with baking parchment a baking tray 18 x 30cm (7 x 12in).

Gently melt the butter, both sugars, cocoa powder and chocolate in a large bowl set over a pan of simmering water. Remove from the heat and leave to stand for 5 minutes.

Then beat in the salt, kirsch and eggs until smooth.

Stir through the flour and cherries and pour into the prepared baking tray. Bake for 30 minutes.

Remove from the oven and place the baking tray into a large roasting tin filled with iced water. This will keep the brownies soft in the centre. Allow to cool completely in the roasting tin.

Whip the cream with the kirsch and icing sugar to form soft peaks. Spread on top of the brownies and dust with icing sugar, cocoa powder and a fresh cherry.

Cut into 10 brownies.

Nibble.

Raspberry Jam Swiss Roll

Makes 6 slices

2 eggs
50g caster sugar
50g plain flour
4 tbsp raspberry jam, warmed
A little caster sugar for dusting

Here's how to make it ...

Preheat the oven to 220°C / 400°F / Gas Mark 7.

Grease and line with baking parchment a baking tray 18 x 30cm (7 x 12in).

Crack the eggs into a mixing bowl and add the caster sugar. Whisk on high speed for 5–10 minutes until the mixture has risen. Write your name in it with the whisk attachment – if it stays visible for a few seconds it's ready.

Carefully fold in the flour with a metal spoon.

Pour into the prepared baking tray and cook in the middle of the oven for 7–10 minutes. Your Swiss roll is ready when the edges of the cake have come away from the sides of the baking tray.

Allow to cool for a few moments before turning out onto a sugared piece of baking parchment that is placed on top of a damp tea towel. Turn the Swiss roll over, remove the paper and cut off the edges.

Spread the warmed raspberry jam over, and then roll your Swiss roll up. Dust with caster sugar.

Cut into 6 slices.

Nibble.

Cherry and Almond Cake

Makes 8 slices

100g blanched almonds
200g butter or margarine, softened
225g caster sugar
3 eggs, beaten
200g self-raising flour
225g glacé cherries, halved
55g flaked almonds

Here's how to make it ...

Preheat the oven to 180°C / 350°F / Gas Mark 4.

Grease and line with baking parchment a deep 20cm (8in) round cake tin.

Place the almonds on a baking tray and toast in the oven for 5 minutes. Whizz them in a food processor until fine.

Cream the butter or margarine and sugar together until light and fluffy. The mixture should fall off a spoon to the count of two.

Add the eggs gradually while mixing together. Then fold in the flour, cherries and ground almonds and transfer to the prepared cake tin. Sprinkle the flaked almonds on top.

Bake for 1 hour 10 minutes until the top is golden and a skewer comes out clean when inserted.

Turn out of the cake tin and allow to cool on a wire rack.

Cut into 8 slices.

Nibble.

Salted Caramel Shortbread

Makes 10 bars

100g caster sugar
Pinch of sea salt flakes
300g butter or margarine, softened
150g caster sugar
350g plain flour
100g rice flour
150g dark chocolate, melted
Sea salt flakes for decoration

Here's how to make it ...

Preheat the oven to 180°C / 350°F / Gas Mark 4.

To make the caramel: heat the caster sugar and sea salt in a pan until golden brown and bubbling. Tip onto an oiled baking sheet on a wooden board. When cool, break into small pieces with a rolling pin.

Beat the butter or margarine and sugar together until light and fluffy.

Add both flours and combine to form a dough.

Put the dough on a lightly floured work surface and shape gently to form a rectangle. Sprinkle with the caramel pieces. Fold in half and place onto a greased and baking parchment-lined baking tray 18 x 30cm (7 x 12in) and push to form an even layer. Cover and refrigerate for 20 minutes.

Bake for 25-30 minutes until golden and cooked through.

Leave to cool in the baking tray for 5 minutes, and then mark 10 bars with a knife and leave to cool completely before cutting through the marked lines.

Cover half of each shortbread piece with melted chocolate and sprinkle some sea salt flakes on top when still wet.

Nibble.

Berry Crumble Traybake

Makes 12 servings

200g mixed fresh or frozen berries

50g caster sugar

2 tbsp cornflour

100g plain flour

70g butter, cut into small cubes

30g caster sugar

Cake

220g plain flour

¾ tsp baking powder

½ tsp cinnamon

50g ground almonds

200g caster sugar

80g butter, softened

2 eggs

40g plain yogurt, mixed with 2 tbsp milk

Here's how to make it ...

Preheat the oven to 180°C / 350°F / Gas Mark 4.

Grease and line a baking tray about 26 x 20cm (10 x 12in) with baking parchment.

Place the fruit and sugar in a pan with 3 tbsp water. Bring just to the boil, reduce the heat and simmer for 2-3 minutes.

Mix the cornflour with a tsp of cold water, add to the fruit and stir until the mixture looks thick. Set aside to cool.

Sieve the 100g of plain flour into a large bowl with the butter and rub gently between your fingertips until it resembles breadcrumbs. Stir in the 30g of caster sugar and set aside.

To make the cake: place all of the ingredients into a large bowl and using an electric whisk, whisk until smooth.

Spoon ⅔ of the mixture into the baking tray, gently pushing it into the corners. Spoon the fruit mixture on top.

Using a teaspoon, dot the remaining cake mixture evenly over the fruit - don't worry if there are little holes - sprinkle over the crumble mixture.

Bake for 45-50 minutes until the crumble topping is golden brown. Remove from the oven, allow to cool in the baking tray and then transfer the cake, with its baking parchment, onto a cooling rack.

Serve with crème fraîche.

Nibble.

Coconut and Lime Slice

Makes 10 squares

200g butter, plus extra for greasing
250g plain flour
30g icing sugar
1 egg

<u>Topping</u>
6 eggs
375g caster sugar
2 tbsp plain flour
2 tbsp cornflour
3 limes, zest and juice
75g desiccated coconut

Here's how to make it ...

Grease and line with baking parchment a baking tray 18 x 30cm (7 x 12in).

Preheat the oven to 180°C / 350°F / Gas Mark 4.

Make the base by placing the butter, flour, icing sugar and egg into a food processor and whizz until a soft dough forms.

Transfer the dough to the baking tray, pushing well into the corners. Cover and refrigerate for 30 minutes.

Bake the base for 20-25 minutes until a pale golden colour.

To make the topping: whisk the eggs, sugar, both flours, lime zest and juice until pale and smooth. Pour over the base and sprinkle coconut on top. The topping should be a thin runny consistency.

Return to the oven and bake for 20-25 minutes until set and lightly golden in colour.

Remove from the oven and allow to cool in the baking tray before cutting into 10 squares.

Nibble.

Coconut Chai Traybake

Makes 10 slices

100ml vegetable oil, plus a little for greasing
250ml coconut milk (less 3 tbsp for topping)
50ml cold tea
4 eggs
2 tsp vanilla extract
4 tbsp ginger syrup (from stem ginger jar)
280g soft brown sugar
250g self-raising flour
75g desiccated coconut
1 tsp each: ground ginger, cinnamon, nutmeg
¼ tsp ground cloves
1 tsp dried cardamom

Topping

3 tbsp coconut milk
120g icing sugar
2 balls of stem ginger, finely chopped
100g pistachios, unsalted, shelled

Here's how to make it ...

Preheat the oven to 180°C / 350°F / Gas Mark 4.

Grease and line with baking parchment a baking tray 18 x 30cm (7 x 12in).

Mix the vegetable oil, coconut milk, tea, eggs, vanilla extract and ginger syrup in a jug. Whisk with a fork to combine.

Place the sugar, flour, coconut and the spices into a large bowl and add the wet ingredients. Whisk to a smooth batter.

Pour the mixture into the baking tray. Bake for 25 minutes until risen and golden; the top should spring back when gently pressed.

Remove from the oven and leave to cool for 15 minutes in the baking tray, and then transfer to a wire rack.

Mix the topping ingredients (except the pistachios) together and drizzle over the top. Scatter with pistachios. Cut into 10 slices.

Nibble.

Baileys Baked Alaska

Makes 8 portions

1 ltr vanilla ice cream
50ml Baileys Irish Cream
1 chocolate cake packet mix
3 egg whites
150g caster sugar

Here's how to make it ...

Make some holes in the ice cream, pour the Baileys over and refreeze for approx. 2-3 hours.

Preheat the oven to 180°C / 350°F / Gas Mark 4. Grease and line with baking parchment a 23cm (9in) round cake tin.

Make the cake mix according to the packet instructions and bake. Turn out and allow to cool on a wire rack.

Whisk the egg whites in a grease free bowl until light and fluffy.

With the mixer on full speed, add the sugar a spoonful at a time.

Put the chocolate cake on a baking tray. Place the ice cream on top and cover with the egg whites ensuring total coverage including the chocolate cake; there must not be any holes.

Bake until golden. Serve immediately.

Nibble.

No-Bake Chocolate Cake

Makes 8 slices

200g milk chocolate, broken into pieces
100g dark chocolate, broken into pieces
110g butter
50g dark Muscovado sugar
120g shortbread biscuits, broken up
110g glacé cherries, chopped
75g hazelnuts
75g pecans
1 small pack Maltesers, broken up

Here's how to make it ...

Line an 18cm (8in) round cake tin with baking parchment.

Melt both chocolates, the butter and sugar in a bowl set over a pan of simmering water.

Stir in the rest of the ingredients and pour into the prepared cake tin. Leave to set.

Remove from the cake tin and cut into 8 slices.

Nibble.

Orange and Cherry Clafoutis

Makes 8 slices

Butter and caster sugar for greasing
100g plain flour
2 eggs
60g caster sugar
200ml milk
¼ tsp vanilla extract
400g cherries, pitted
1 orange, grated zest and juice
1 tbsp Cointreau liqueur
Icing sugar to dust

Here's how to make it ...

Preheat the oven to 180°C / 350°F / Gas Mark 4.

Grease a 25cm (10in) round baking or quiche dish with butter, and then cover in caster sugar.

Put the flour, eggs, caster sugar, milk and vanilla extract into a blender. Blend until smooth. Cover and leave to rest for 30 minutes in the fridge.

Place the cherries on the baking dish and put in the oven for 5 minutes to soften.

Meanwhile, add the orange zest and juice, and the Cointreau liqueur to the batter; mix thoroughly.

Remove the dish from the oven, pour the batter over the cherries and return to the oven for about 30 minutes until puffy and golden.

Dust with icing sugar.

Nibble.

Thank you …

Julie, Angela, Neil, Robert, Mick and all at Sirdar - your love for yarn is infectious and your help with pattern writing from design concept to final copy so thorough. You are a fantastic team to work with, thank you.

An author is only as good as the editor, thank you for the many hours of attention to detail and consistency Michelle. Late night discussions on FaceTime with cloud editing will never be the same again!

Work should be fun, and that's certainly true when you work with Anders Beier photography: Anders and Sune, thank you for a fantastic creative journey. Thorstein Robert, thank you for your post-production.

Paul, thank you for your idea about the book and for your encouragement to get me out of my man cave and back to life. We may be miles apart, but our friendship is close. Also, Karen and Simon, long live the class of '96.

To my Knitters and Nibblers, Stu and his team at The Peckham Pelican. Loyalty, laughs and friends, you are a phenomenal group.

Tom and Henry Harrap, the founders of Sirdar and the home of Great British knitting, thank you for your vision.

Thank you Margaret, my mum, for teaching me to knit and proofreading my work. I'm sorry I gave you a jumper for your birthday and the sleeves the following Christmas. Ingrid, my mother-in-law, our friendship is so precious to me, as is the efficacy of using circular needles. Thank you for teaching me.

My dear friends who have allowed me to knit at parties and tolerated all sorts of garments bestowed upon them, thank you. Special thanks also goes to Alan and Marcus, Neil, Charlie and Katrina. Not forgetting Edouard and Edouard for always encouraging me.

Lastly, but most importantly. Thomas - thank you for putting up with many #balls of wool at home.

To Olly, David, Keiren, Richard, Ali, Connor, Emma, Neil, Lorna, Liz, Rob, Mike and of course, Debbieanne: strike a pose, there's nothing to it.

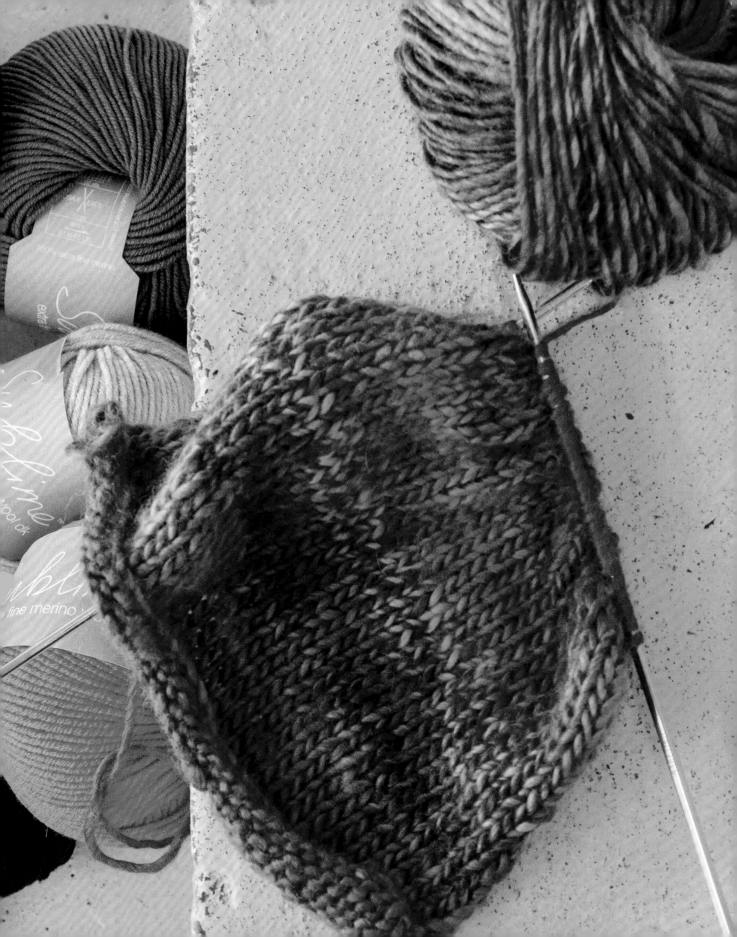

About the Authors

James McIntosh MA

A farmer's son from Northern Ireland who lives in the *'posh part'* of Peckham, London. Regular food TV presenter in China and multi Gourmand World Award-winning food writer and obsessive knitter.

jamesmcintosh.co.uk

Michelle Brachet MA

Gourmand World Award-winning drinks writer, cognac and food consultant and educator. Food, drink and lifestyle book editor.

michellebrachet.co.uk

Dr Thomas A. Ernst FRCP

Senior Consultant Doctor in a large teaching hospital in central London, specialising in elderly care and mindfulness within a clinical setting.

drternst.com

Anders Beier

Winner of the title of Gourmand *'Best Food Photographer in the World'* for 2 years running, founder and director of the Njord Sustainable Food Photography Competition with Sune Rasborg.

andersbeier.com

Sune Rasborg

Gourmand World Award-winning food stylist and chef, father of 2, Danish food TV presenter.

sunerasborg.com

WHAT HAPPENS IN
KNITTING CLUB
STAYS IN KNITTING CLUB

Knit and Nibble Time

Every other week in Peckham, South East London, James runs Knit and Nibble Time at The Peckham Pelican.

A fun group of knitters from all walks of life come together; they learn from each other, laugh and knit and nibble together.

It's not a precious or pressurised kind of knitting group: it is sociable, relaxed, rewarding and enjoyable.

For more information on dates, times and special events, visit knitnibble.com

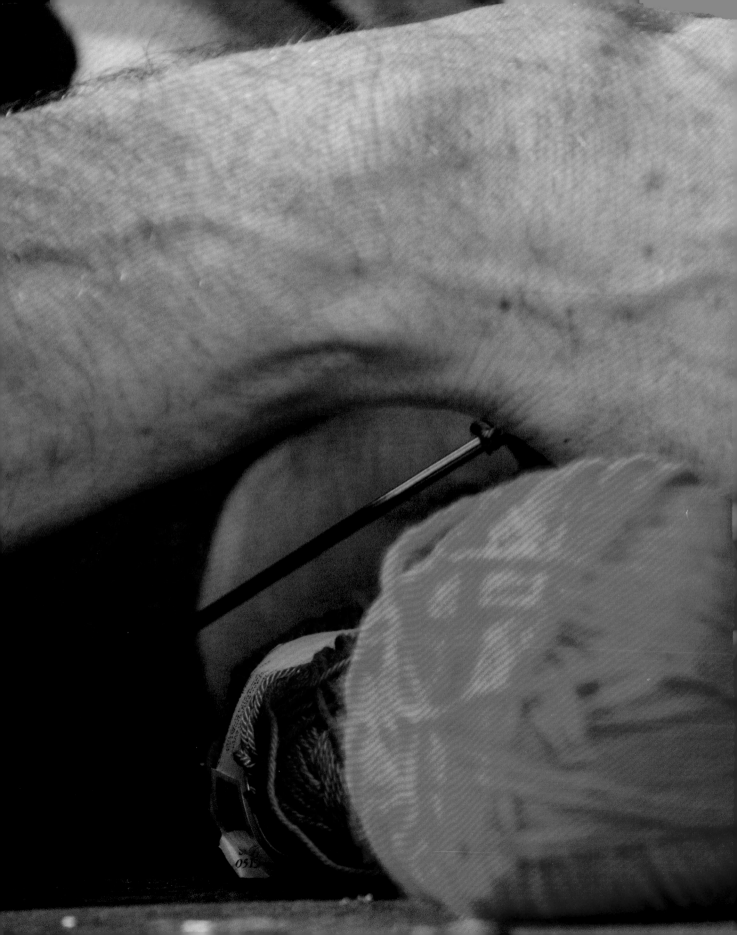

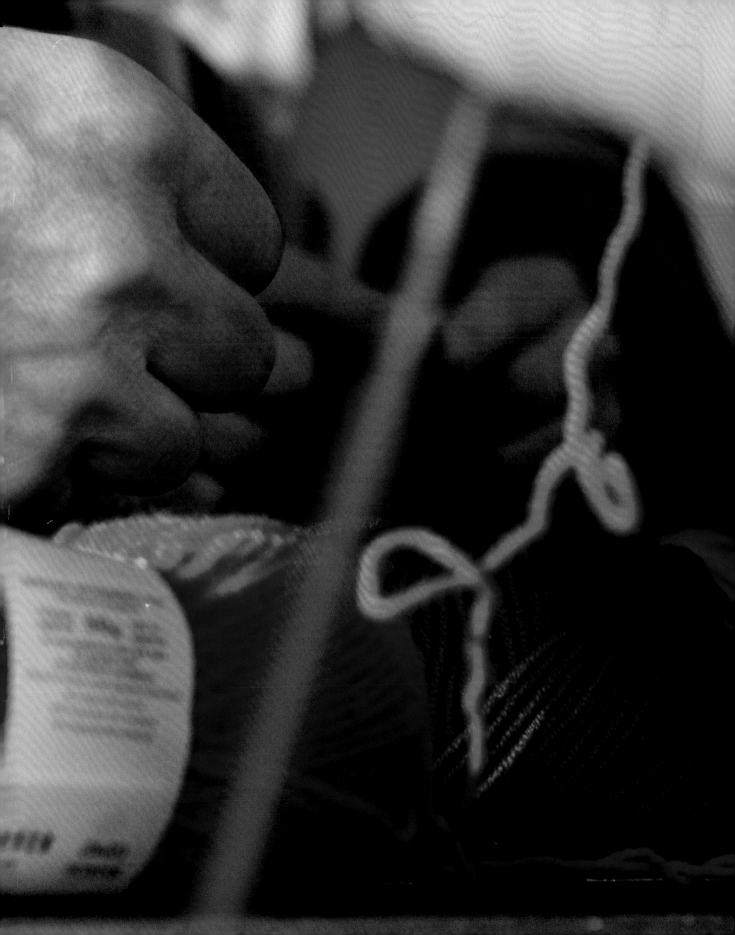